# GOSPEL EARTH

## Steven Patrick

ISBN 978-1-0980-5925-5 (paperback)
ISBN 978-1-0980-7627-6 (hardcover)
ISBN 978-1-0980-5926-2 (digital)

Christian Faith Publishing, Inc.
832 Park Avenue
Meadville, PA 16335
www.christianfaithpublishing.com

Printed in the United States of America

# INTRODUCTION

*For the word of God is living and powerful, and sharper than any two-edged sword, piercing even to the division of soul and spirit, and of joints and marrow, and is a discerner of the thoughts and intents of the heart.*

*Hebrews 4:12*

—

These words are found in the Christian Bible. This verse and many others like it declare that God's Word is true and everlasting. Most people professing to be Christians today say that they believe everything that is written in the Bible is true, but do they really? Have a majority of believers actually read the whole book from Genesis to Revelation? I have exhaustively studied and poured over what is actually between the pages of our bibles, collecting dust on the shelfs of millions of homes, and the truths that have been discovered are absolutely astonishing.

*Gospel Earth* does not seek to start controversy, but the truths that are hidden in plain sight will affect every church and every believer. This book is not specifically a Christian book, nor is it a secular book, but it is a book of fundamental truths that are utterly amazing. It is a book for anyone with questions, for people who desire a deeper knowledge, for people who know that something is not right—and above all—want the truth free from lies and agendas.

These words before you will spark truth in the hearts and minds of mankind, and for some, it will change everything.

It is unique in the regard that each human who reads it will have to choose which side they are on; there is no room for fence-sitters. This book calls out the lies that we live with daily, and it calls it out everyone from the atheist to the hardcore Christian. Being a Christian means believing in the Bible and believing all of it with your heart and mind. Being an atheist means to not believe in God—a rejection of God. Atheism is contrasted with theism, which, in its most general form, is the belief that God does exist. Christian, atheist, and anyone who thinks that they are in between, the words you read from here on out will cause you to fall on one side or the other.

Besides the Bible, you will never read another book like this in your lifetime. Get ready to swallow the red pill and be exposed to everything. It is with supreme confidence that these words were written. The facts that are laid out within these pages are indisputable and will give the Atheist and the Christian enough ammunition to take a firm stand for their side, but who will win?

There are basic facts of life that are not ever talked about that contain the answers to "*who we are*" as humans and what we believe to be true. So "*true*" and engrained are these "*facts*" in every human throughout our world that being on the other side of a simple question can be dangerous and all for not thinking like the masses. Group thinking is a tremendous source of power for the ones deciding what the group will think.

Here is the first spoiler alert: the masses are never right. It is always the smaller groups that strive to stand for the right reasons and the just causes that wins the day, always in contrast against the masses. The ideas discussed in this book are taboo to most of humanity and not allowed to be spoken of among a huge portion of the population, including our school systems, churches, politics, careers, and mundane daily conversations. The year is 2020, but 1984 has finally shown up...and this is not science fiction. We have not yet evolved into being able to examine the lies and corruption that is being forced down the public's throats, ears, eyes, and minds in the most diabolical of ways, and it is frightening, to say the least. "Right reasons" and "just causes" are exiled as nonsense because some thoughts can't be talked about no matter how interesting and thought provoking the ideas may be even if it's truth. Something is not right.

The level of derision surrounding the topic of this book stems from the atheist and the Christian, and they are united. This is not dramatic or wishful thinking in attempts to spark controversy and to sell a book. This is a serious issue and a thoughtful book for an enlightened and educated society, which may or may not be prepared for the information found between its pages. Again, regardless of which side you fall, you will be affected, and it will change your life.

Know this: when the other side of an argument turns to hate and violence and your side has all but disowned you, a very serious nerve has been struck. There is no doubt that this book will be ostracized by all sides because we dare to ask the question, but we ask none the less. Will we follow the masses? Do we believe what we believe? And what do we really believe?

Since childhood and our earliest days of education we were taught worldly theories that go against what the Bible teaches. Example: we were taught the theory of evolution as fact. This book is not about evolution, but as a matter of record, Christians don't believe in that theory yet it was taught to us as fact when we were young and impressionable children, and when you are taught something at a young age that is false and everyone around you, including trusted adults, believe it; that can truly be classified as "programming" or "brainwashing." Furthermore, as we grow older and mature, these "facts" that we were taught as children are then reinforced in adulthood. There is no questioning them, and if you do, you are forcefully reprogrammed by the masses in the form of ridicule and assault—verbally and possibly physically.

The history of human nature indicates that we don't want to be singled out. We want to be liked and respected. We want to fit in and be successful in life, so most people go along with certain ideas and theories because to question them is considered ignorance, which in turn leads to failure. Overcoming this kind of "programming" re-enforced by negative reaction is near impossible. If you dare to question, if you dare to argue, if you dare to stand against the conventional "wisdom" of the masses, the group thinkers will be mindful of you.

With that dower set up and doomsday attitude, you may ask, why write a book about such a topic? I've asked myself that a thousand times: is it worth it? Obviously, I think so. Even in the Christian world where love is supposed to conquer all, this book will be slandered. It will be criticized and dismissed from both sides of the isle. When you anger all sides with an original thought, then you're on to something. The words of this book will open eyes, will cause questions to be asked, and will demand answers. There is no turning back. Once a truth is presented and digested by thoughtful deep thinkers, life will change for us all. To answer the question, this book was written because it had to be. Those who have ears, let them hear.

# CHAPTER 1

## The Bible, As We Know It

*In the beginning God created the heavens and the earth.*

*—Genesis 1:1*

At the very start of this book, I want it understood that I am no pastor—nor am I an expert in Hebrew, Latin, or Greek. I am also not an expert on the Bible, philosophy, science, history, or mathematical calculations. Having said that, the reader should know that I have read the entire Bible multiple times and I am a lover of God's Word and consider myself a born-again believer in the Christian faith with a firm grasp of the Christian doctrines.

I am a husband and a father. I am also Papa to my grandchildren. I am fifty-five years old this year, and I recently retired. My wife and I worked hard to raise our kids and to provide a nice life for them. We live a modest life in a nice neighborhood in California, our entire family was born and raised here. I have studied the New King James Bible along with the King James Bible and cross-referenced with many other versions of the Bible in the writing of this book. The Greek and Hebrew definitions of many words used in the original translations have been verified using *Strong's Concordance,* Irwin's concordance, Cruden's commentary, *Nelson's Bible Dictionary*, and many other resources. This does not make me an expert, it simply means that I am capable of simple research and that I seek knowledge and understanding. I am a Christian of forty-five-plus years who seeks truth in hopes of laying out a solid defense of what the Word of God is telling us in almost every book that is included in the Bible as we know it today.

I believe that knowledge is power and that the truth will set you free (*John 8:32*) and that in the beginning God created (*Genesis 1:1*) My pastor has said more than once that this is the start of the Christian faith: we must believe that God created this world for us.

I was taught that the Bible is 100 percent accurate, backed up by the oldest known scrolls (the Dead Sea Scrolls) along with archeological findings of the past and continuing finds every year that only confirm that what is in the Bible is true.

It has been estimated that 65 percent of Americans consider themselves to be of the Christian faith. If that is true, then a majority of you were most likely taught that the Christian Bible is accurate. As Christians, we base our faith and trust in God's Word and the accuracy of it. If you are a nonbeliever and you've never read the Bible, you should at least know the first line in the book. It is this: "*In the beginning God created the heavens and the earth.*" *Genesis 1:1*. The Bible, being the best-selling book of all time, has had its opening line quoted and read more than any other words in all of literature.

The Bible clearly says that "[i]*n the beginning God created*" This is basic Christianity. As Christians, we believe this. Why do we believe this? Is it because it is what we were taught by people of influence when we were young? Programming can go both ways. Have we been programmed by the world and the Christian faith? Does the world's view mesh with what the Bible says or are they in unreconcilable conflict? How does science and observation, experiments, sense, and experience come together? Can they come together? Who's right when it comes to the big questions about life on earth, and who is lying? Because someone is lying.

Since time began, man has wondered about these big questions. How did the earth get here? Are we flying through space, and if so, how? Are we spinning around at a thousand miles per hour like we were taught? Was there a Big Bang? Did we evolve from some primordial soup? If these "facts" are not correct, were we then lied to? And was it done on purpose?

As a born-again Christian, I believe that God created all, including science and natural laws. I don't trust the world, and I don't trust an education system that is run by a government that does not have any interest in supporting the Christian faith. I do trust in the Bible. I believe that the Bible is truth and I believe that every story in the Bible is also truth. I believe that every word is perfectly placed just as God wanted it placed. If I did not believe this, then I would not be a Christian and this book would have never been written. This book is relying on the premise that the Bible is 100 percent accurate. So if you believe that, then we are of like mind. If you don't, then read on to see if the Christian faith really believes in what it says it believes in or if we too, are liars.

I will assume that I am writing mostly to Bible-believing, born-again Christians, and if you are not, then it is my hope and prayer that you will become a born-again believer by asking God to come live in your heart and save your soul from hell by accepting God's free gift that He gave us by having his only son die in our place and take what we deserved so that we may escape the punishment of our sin. This is Christianity. Read *Romans 10:8–13, John 3:16, and Ephesians 2:8–9.*

Once you become a believer, it is very important to know what it is you believe in. Under the assumption that most people reading this book are believers, I ask the question, what do you know about God's Word? Have you studied it? Do you read the Bible daily? If you want to grow in knowledge and love for our Lord, this is necessary. God gives us all the answers to life in his Holy Word, but He won't force us to read it. We must do our part.

Ignorance is no excuse.

Believing lies because it's easier than the hassle of defending the Bible tugs at the very soul of the Christian, and we have been lied to past the point of incredulity.

So then, what does God's Word say after "in the beginning"? The very first pages of any good book will give you some of the best insight into its author. The author wants you to keep reading; he or she wants to sell books. If you're bored with the first few pages, why would you go further? This author certainly hopes that you are intrigued enough to continue reading this book. Well then, let's get to it!

What is this book about? It's all about the validity of God's Word. Can it be trusted? Are there mistakes? Are there outright lies? If you've been a born-again Christian for any amount of time, I'm sure that you've gone to a Bible-believing church with a Bible-believing, and a Bible-teaching pastor. I have been faithfully attending such churches for fifty years. While that makes me old, it has also exposed God's Word to me throughout my entire life.

I've had several pastors throughout the years, and I believe that they were and are men of God, preaching and teaching with a holy reverence that was and is their calling. I love these men, and I thank them with everything in me for showing me truth and helping me to lead myself and my family to the blessed assurance of our salvation. How blessed are the feet of the preacher. However, I am positive that few, if any, of these pastors will agree with what I have found to be absolute truth in the pages of God's Word.

There it is, the teaser, and you had to read a little further than you thought. Thank you for not giving up, further set up is necessary, but rest assured that in a few pages, you will know where all this is going.

I've read plenty of books through the first few pages standing in the local bookstore, and a lot of them I didn't buy because if you don't have me intrigued by page three, I'm most likely putting the book back on the shelf.

Non-Christians, please keep reading. There is a lot in here that you will find most interesting too. Regardless, I will assume that 90 percent of people reading this book are already born-again believers. I'm sure as a Bible-believing Christian, you have had at least some experience in reading the Bible—maybe at church as the pastor asks you to turn to a passage or in your own home study and quiet time.

Truthfully, I have not always been the guy to make sure that I looked at God's Word on a daily basis for much of my life, but I can tell you that when I make it a priority to read His Word daily (which

I now have done for a long time) it has a huge impact on my day and week and month and year. Have you ever read a passage that maybe you've read in the past or maybe even have memorized only to find a new meaning in it at a second, third, or even fourth reading? God's Word comes to us as we read and as we need. It is truly the Living Word. I'm not the best at memorizing scripture, but the more you read His Word, the more you'll be amazed at what is retained in your mind. I challenge you to read it daily, and I challenge you to study and look deep into what the words of our Holy Bibles are actually saying in addition and simultaneously while reading this author's words. I strongly suggest this. As you read this book, get your Bible out and examine it next to *Gospel Earth*. We make no excuse for error as God's Word is supposed to be flawless, and the words of this book should be scrutinized alongside the Bible. If *Gospel Earth* goes against the Bible, then it is wrong, but if these words agree with the Bible, then it can be assumed that they are correct.

We are all in this world together, and we all need to know basic things in order to survive in it. If for instance we were taught the wrong meaning of words when we were young, how messed up would we be trying to function in this world as adults? If we were taught as young children that we could fly like the birds if we get high enough, we might believe it because persons of authority that we trust wouldn't lie to us, would they? If we witnessed people jump off a tall building to test this theory, I'm sure that the line for "flying" would shrink immediately and our faith in the adults would be severely questioned. It is obvious that most of today's Christians have indeed taken a jump off of Bible-based facts and into a pool of lies.

What is about to be spelled out won't make me many friends and has, quite frankly, upset more than one of my own family members. I, however, do not apologize for truth. The very first page of the Bible would turn brother against brother and friend against friend if its true meaning were open to debate in the church and the secular world. That is actually a big source of disappointment in my own life—that I cannot discuss or even debate the truth that I speak of even among good Christian friends. It is also why I wrote this book. This is that debate. Why have I potentially alienated friends and family? What could be so important to cause friction in not only my family but in my beloved church family? Money? Fame? Recognition? Would any of that even be it worth it? No. But for truth, faith, and our Lord. One must say yes, it is worth it, and I would gladly put my reputation and my life at risk for my Savior. What has been found in the scriptures challenges everything I thought I knew, and it will challenge you as well.

Does God's Word teach us 100 percent truth all the time on every page of the Bible?

If you read the very first chapter of the Bible, you have read how the author describes the world in which we live—the world that the Creator Himself built for us. It is a matter of historical record for the believer. If you are studious and know your Bible, you know that it was Moses who wrote the first five books of our Bible, and for extra credit, you would also realize that Moses was not alive when the events of Genesis took pace, the very first book of the Bible. Knowing these basic Christian facts, it has probably dawned on you that God had to tell Moses exactly what to write, word for word, because again, Moses was not an eyewitness.

God told Moses, and Moses wrote. This is also true of all the other books in the Bible from Genesis to Revelation. As Christians, we believe that all scripture is inspired by God and therefore approved by God. And God does not make mistakes—whether written by man or not.

The big set up is this: it is my firm and unwavering belief that God's Word teaches us something in His very first book of Genesis that goes against a most fundamental "truth" that we have been taught since childhood and that we think we know beyond any shadow of doubt.

In *Genesis 15:12*, God stated, "*Now when the sun was going down a deep sleep fell upon Abram; and behold, horror and great darkness fell upon him.*" This verse indicates movement of the sun by saying that it was going down. But we were taught the sun does not move, that we rotate and spin around it because of gravity. Were you as shocked as I? Well, there it is! No need to read any further. You're probably not as inspired as I was and may even be thinking, *This guy is a nut job, a kook. Probably thinks the earth is flat too.* Please don't give up, this is God's Word. Prove this nut job wrong and prove that the Bible is right. Okay, one verse, big deal. You will need more convincing than that, so here are a couple of other verses to consider.

> And it came to pass *after the sun went down* and it was dark, that behold, there appeared a smoking oven and a burning torch that passed between those pieces. (Genesis 15:17)

> *The sun had risen upon the earth* when Lot entered Zoar. (Genesis 19:23)

Two more verses in the first book confirming that the sun moves. Again, that's not what we were taught. We were taught that the earth spins around the sun and that the sun is stationary. If you're a Christian or non-Christian, you must ask, does the Bible lie? What is this that we or they believe in? Is the Bible wrong in the very first book on the very first page? It's been argued that flawed men wrote the Bible and that man must have wrote what man perceived to be true. Moses probably thought, *Well, it looks like the sun is moving, so that's what I will write!*

When it comes to God's Word, I don't care for words like *probably* and *maybe.* I don't like the words *probably* and *maybe* anywhere let alone in the Bible! And please remember, God was telling Moses what to write. Did God get it wrong? It would be a good idea for you to read the first chapter of Genesis before going further to refresh the creation story in your mind before reading on. Did you notice how eloquent the writing is throughout the very first book?

We were created to be tremendously intelligent! We were not cavemen. That being true, I'm sure I'm not going to undo your firm belief in what you were taught as a child. This is something called cognitive dissonance, and that will be explained later in greater detail. There are many more verses to come. Let's just say as an atheist, these would just be some of the needed verses to attack the Christian faith and all one would need to win a debate with silly Christians.

"Your Bible says the sun moves!"

"You are stupid, and you are wrong!"

This is the only argument for the nonbeliever that he or she would ever need because everyone knows beyond any shadow of doubt that the earth spins and the sun stands still. That is, unless you are armed with the truth, and God's Word is that truth and it always will be.

God is real. If you don't believe that, put this book down and pray to this "unreal" God to show Himself to you, and He will show you just how real He is. Satan is also real. And he is scary as hell. The Bible teaches us in Genesis chapter 3, where Satan is first introduced, that the serpent is the most cunning of all the beasts. The first thing the devil did was lie so that he could corrupt mankind at the very beginning of our existence. This lie cost mankind dearly for the rest of our time here on this earth. Work became hard, bearing children became painful, and death entered our world—all because of pride and lies. We wanted to be like God, not satisfied with our new life if it had any restrictions. If you're a good parent or had good parents, you'll realize at some point that they loved you and placed restrictions on you to keep you safe just as I did with my own children. We have been put on restriction. Bottom line is we did this to ourselves and we live with the consequences of our sins daily.

If you don't remember, Satan told Eve, the first woman, that God had lied to her and Adam. God loved the first man and woman He ever created just as he loves each and every person ever born and would not and is, in fact, incapable of lying. Satan taught us to lie, and it is us that rejects God's perfect love. Eve took the bait and passed it on to Adam, and Adam in turn had the nerve to blame God for giving him the woman. Just like man, right? Notice, men, that we didn't even try to defend the weaker vessel, and Satan went right after her. God gave us a perfect helpmate, and we turned on her at the first sign of confrontation. Let's hope that we've evolved into a higher understanding of God's infinite love for us as humans. After all, He made us in His image. So one moment, we were walking and talking with the Creator of all, and the next, we sinned and were kicked out of Eden to toil on the earth for the rest of our history.

Adam was extremely intelligent; the Bible tells us that God had him name all the animals. Just look at an elephant and try to think of a better name description. But smart Adam screwed up and then tried to blame God and here we are today.

Satan was and still is very cunning. It is my firm belief that he has tried to corrupt everything God has made holy, including God's Word. He is after all extremely anti-God. Pride being a huge problem that leads to the most destruction, and it is what got him kicked out of heaven in the first place. Pride is also the biggest reason that people don't want to admit that they are wrong about anything.

"I am not wrong, I am right!"

"You can't tell me what to do! Who do you think you are?"

"You're ignorant, and I will not waste my time entertaining your wacky theories."

Whose wacky theories? I didn't write the Bible.

My Bible is a New King James version and I love it. It is made of soft dark leather, has the red print of Jesus's words in the New Testament and big letters that I can see well with my glasses on. As far as I know, it is an approved Bible that I bought in a Christian bookstore. I take it to church every week and study from it at home. In that Bible in the New Testament found in the book of *Matthew*, Jesus (the Creator who spoke all things into existence—see *John 1:1*) says in chapter 5 verse 45 that *"He makes His sun rise on the evil and the good."*

Okay, well, there you have it again! Is the Bible wrong again? We now have the Creator of everything, The Son, saying that the sun moves. Jesus claims ownership of the sun as well by using the phrase "His sun." Jesus didn't make a mistake, He got it right and said just what He wanted to say, the way He wanted to say it.

# CHAPTER 2

# The Sun

*And you shall know the truth and the truth shall set you free.*

*—John 8:32*

We are going to delve into God's Word. So as we weave ourselves through the Bible, let's start with the logical position, the beginning, and see what Genesis tells us about the world we live in.

In Genesis, the word *earth* is used twenty times in thirty-one verses of the first chapter. God Himself gave our world that name in verse 10 of the first chapter. It's quite a unique word, and there is no other word quite like it.

*First,* God said, "Let there be light" and there was light and God saw that it was good. This is God's light and not the light of the sun because the sun had yet to be made.

*Second,* God divided the waters from the waters and created what He calls the firmament. This statement also infers that waters were pre-existing, an interesting thought to ponder. Do yourself a favor, and Google the word *firmament* and see what it says. Wikipedia describes the word *firmament* as a protective structure. Protecting from what? According to the Word of God, from waters above. *Merriam-Webster's* states it is "the vault or arch of the sky." It

16

goes on to say that it is in the heavens. The example sentence given is this, "The stars twinkled in the firmament."

*"Praise Him the waters that be above heaven" (Psalm 148:4).*

*Third*, God caused dry land to appear where there was none and called it earth.

*Fourth*, God created life on this new earth in the form of grass, herbs, and seeds. "The giant oak rests in the acorn." Think about the complexities inside of that sentence. The magnitude and the wonderful intricacies of that is an example to be in awe of. God then created the sun, the moon, and the stars and put them in the firmament, as *Merriam-Webster* already pointed out to us.

These things were to be used for signs and seasons. Two individual lights to guide the day and the night. Perfect symmetry. Perfect mathematical equation to last forever.

*Fifth*, God created all living creatures in the waters. Life has changed now. The earth and its waters were filled with creatures of the deep—some of which we've seen, others that are of the past, and more that are to come.

*Sixth*, God created all animals of the land and of the air—now breathing oxygen and not water. An entirely new concept. A new form of creature. His creation, evolved, if you would, and then finally He created his crowing jewel. His most amazing thing yet—us. Mankind. Men and women, made in His image and glory, created to reflect His majesty. In this above all other things did He feel complete and full love. Love is the meaning of everything. God loves, so God created, and he created a way for eternal creation.

Think about your body. Your eyes, your vital organs, your muscular system, your skeletal system, your nervous system, all your senses, and how they interact with your storehouse of everything that is your brain—compiled into a mass that God pulled from dirt and began to work out truth and perfection into being. He did this through Adam, and He did it again through Jesus Christ. This is the God of the Bible; God is love.

Oh, and He did it all in six days (literal twenty-four hour days just as we know time today).

Finally, on the *seventh* day, He rested from His work and declared the day to be holy and blessed for all the good He created.

So that is the history and order in which God created everything according to the Bible. It is important to remind ourselves that it is still Moses writing these words, given to him by God Himself. Now granted, some scholars believe that Genesis had multiple authors that maybe even included the first man Adam himself, but regardless of the author, in order to believe this account, you would have to acknowledge that whoever did in fact write these words was not present at the time and could only detail the words God relayed to Him in the language that he knew, Hebrew. What we do know is that whomever the editor of Genesis was, they were led by the Spirit to write exactly what God wanted said.

As already mentioned I've been going to church for over fifty years, I know all the stories backwards and forwards. I must have heard the story of the prodigal son at least fifty times. I know about the thief on the cross, the parting of an ocean where people walked on dry land, the widows mite, Noah's ark where two of every animal loaded onto a massive boat to save the animals and the human race, water being turned into wine, feeding ten thousand people with very little food and then having leftovers, the blind being given sight, the lame made to walk, a man being swallowed by a great fish and then living in it for three days, rivers turned into blood, frogs falling from the sky, a woman giving birth at ninety, men living to almost a thousand years old, the sun being stopped, a talking donkey, a virgin birth, and people rising from the dead! The stories are profound! They are outrageous! They are unprecedented and bold! The world says you'd have to be a lunatic to believe those things.

Knowing and believing all of these stories is what the Christian faith is composed of, but I have never once heard a sermon on the topic of the very first page of the Bible in great detail.

Where are the sermons about our magnificent earth that God built for us and basing it strictly out of the Bible? Without any need for extra nonbiblical texts. He devoted six days of constant creation and unparalleled genius to create a perfect place with a perfect system that no act of randomness could produce, and yet we debate politics from the pulpit rather than the truth that is Creation.

> *"For the invisible things of him from the creation of the world are clearly seen, being understood by the things that are made, even his eternal power and Godhead; so that they are without excuse"* (Romans 1:20).

*Without excuse.* We don't need to make excuses about who it is we are sourcing. The Word of God needs no other reproof, and all other things can be decided upon looking at His wonders. All things are revealed through creation and not man. There are men far greater in wisdom and knowledge than I that can admit to simply looking at the complexity of life and our world and knowing that we do not know.

The various pastors we've been under for all these years have to be more learned than us, right? It's their job to study the scriptures and teach us from them. But the Word of God must be wrong if all our pastors disagree with it. You have to say that either the Bible is lying or something very sinister has been going on for a very long time to keep us uninformed.

This is the fundamental argument of this book. Is the Bible right or is the world? Has your mind been challenged so far or at the very least intrigued. The few verses given are enough to rest the case but might be a little underwhelming for the unimpressed.

So here are a few more. Bust out your Bible and follow along. Allow the Word of God to make its way into your heart and ask for truth and understanding. For those that ask, receive.

Please get your Bible out and read along. Space has been left for note taking.

> But when the *sun was up* they were scorched, and because they had no root they withered away. (Matthew 13:6)

Your commanders are like swarming locusts, and your generals like great grasshoppers, which camp in the hedges on a cold day; when the *sun rises* they flee away, and the place where they are is not known. (Nahum 3:17)

In them He has set a tabernacle for the sun, which is like a bridegroom coming out of his chamber, and rejoices like a strong man to run its race. *Its rising* is from one end of heaven, and its *circuit* to the other end; and there is nothing hidden from its heat. (Psalm 19:5–6)

The *sun also rises*, and the *sun goes down*, and hastens to the place where it arose. (Ecclesiastes 1:5)

He appointed the moon for seasons; the *sun knows it's going down.* (Psalm 104:19)

When the *sun rises*, they gather together, and lie down in their dens. (Psalm 104:22)

Your *sun shall no longer go down*, nor shall your moon withdraw itself; for the Lord will be your everlasting light, and the days of your mourning shall be ended. (Isaiah 60:20)

He commands the *sun, and it does not rise*; He seals off the stars. (Job 9:7)

Then Joshua spoke to the Lord in the day when the Lord delivered up the Amorites before the children of Israel, and he said in the sight of Israel: *"Sun, stand still* over Gibeon; and moon, in the Valley of Aijalon. So the *sun stood still,* and the moon stopped, till the people had revenge upon their enemies. (Joshua 10:12–13)

*The sun and the moon stood still* in their habitation; at the light of your arrows they went, at the shining of your glittering spear. (Habakkuk 3:11)

And when the *sun goes down*, he shall be clean; and afterward he may eat the holy offerings, because it is his food. (Leviticus 22:7)

But at the place where the Lord your God chooses to make His name abide, there you shall sacrifice the Passover at twilight, at the *going down of the sun*, at the time you came out of Egypt. (Deuteronomy 16:6)

So it was at the time of *the going down of the sun* that Joshua commanded, and they took them down from the trees, cast them into the cave where they had been hidden, and laid large stones against the cave's mouth, which remain until this very day. (Joshua 10:27)

The *sun had risen* upon the earth when Lot entered Zoar. (Genesis 19:23)

Therefore you shall have night without vision, and you shall have darkness without divination; *the sun shall go down* on the prophets, and the day shall be dark for them. (Micah 3:6)

When the *sun was setting*, all those who had any that were sick with various diseases brought them to Him; and He laid His hands on every one of them and healed them. (Luke 4:40)

Be angry, and do not let the *sun go down* on your wrath. (Ephesians 4:26)

For no sooner has the *sun risen* with a burning heat than it withers the grass; its flower falls, and its beautiful appearance perishes. So the rich man also will fade away in his pursuits. (James 1:11)

Very early in the morning, on the first day of the week, they came to the tomb when the *sun had risen.* (Mark 16:2)

But Moses' hands became heavy; so they took a stone and put it under him, and he sat on it. And Aaron and Hur supported his hands, one on one side, and his hands were steady until the *going down of the sun.* (Exodus 17:12)

At evening, when the *sun had set,* they brought to Him all who were sick and those who were demon-possessed. (Mark 1:32)

Just as he crossed over Penuel, *the sun rose* on him, and he limped on his hip. (Genesis 32:31)

For He makes *His sun rise* on the evil and on the good, and sends rain on the just and on the unjust. (Matthew 5:45)

But when the *sun was up* it was scorched, and because it had no root it withered away. (Mark 4:6)

These are the kings of the land whom the children of Israel defeated, and whose land they possessed on the other side of the Jordan toward the *rising of the sun*, from the river Arnon to mount Herman, and all the eastern plain. (Joshua 12:1)

"And it shall come to pass in that day," says the Lord God, "that I will make the *sun go down* at noon, and I will darken the earth in broad daylight." (Amos 8:9)

"She languishes who has borne seven; she has breathed her last; her *sun has gone down* while it was yet day; she has been ashamed and confounded. And the remnant of them I will deliver to the sword before their enemies," says the Lord. (Jeremiah 15:9)

And the king of Ai he hanged on a tree until evening. And as soon as the *sun was down*, Joshua commanded that they should take his corpse down from the tree, cast it at the entrance of the gate of the city, and raise over it a great heap of stones that remains to this day. (Joshua 8:29)

The mighty one, God the Lord, has spoken and called the earth, from the *rising of the sun* to its *going down*. (Psalm 50:1)

The battle increased that day, and the king of Israel propped himself up in his chariot facing the Syrians until evening; and about the time of *sunset* he died. (2 Chronicles 18:34)

Then, as the *sun was going down*, a shout went throughout the army, saying, "Every man to his city, and every man to his own country!" (1 Kings 22:36)

And he shall be like the light of the morning when the *sun rises*, a morning without clouds, like the tender grass springing out of the earth, by clear shining after rain. (2 Samuel 23:4)

Joab and Abishai also pursued Abner, and when the *sun was going down* when they came to the hill of Ammah, which is before Giah by the road to the wilderness of Gibeon. (2 Samuel 2:24)

And they passed by and went their way; and the *sun went down* on them near Gibeath, which belongs to Benjamin. (Judges 19:14)

Then from Sarid it went eastward toward the *sunrise* along the border of Chisloth Tabor, and went out toward Daberath, bypassing Japhia. (Joshua 19:12)

So the men of the city said to him on the seventh day before the *sun went down*: "What is stronger than a lion?" And he said to them, "If you had not plowed my heifer, you would not have solved my riddle!" (Judges 14:18)

It turned toward the *sunrise* to Beth Dagon; and it reached to Zebulun and to the Valley of Jiphthah El, then northward beyond Beth Emek and Neiel, bypassing Cabul which was on the left. (Joshua 19:27)

Are they not on the other side of the Jordan, toward the *setting sun*, in the land of the Canaanites who dwell in the plain opposite Gilgal, beside the terebinth trees of Moreh? (Deuteronomy 11:30)

If the *sun has risen* on him, there shall be guilt for his bloodshed. (Exodus 22:3)

And it shall be, as soon as the *sun is up* in the morning, that you shall rise early and rush upon the city; and when he and the people who are with them come against you, you may then do to them as you find opportunity. (Judges 9:33)

You shall return to the land of your possession and enjoy it, which Moses the Lords servant gave you on this side of the Jordan toward the *sunrise*. (Joshua 1:15)

From the wilderness and this Lebanon as far as the great river, the River Euphrates, all the land of the Hittites, and to the great sea toward the *going down of the sun*, shall be your territory. (Joshua 1:4)

Thus let all your enemies perish, O Lord. But let those who love Him be like the *sun when it comes out* in full strength. (Judges 5:31)

For the stars of heaven and their constellations will not give their light. The *sun* will be darkened in its *going forth*, and the *moon* will not cause *its light* to shine. (Isaiah 13:10)

| Book and Verse | Emphasized Phraseology | Greek/ Hebrew | Definition |
|---|---|---|---|
| Matthew 13:6 | "When the sun was up" | An'-o | Verb: Upward, above, High |
| Nahum 3:17 | "When the sun rises" | zaw-rakh' | Verb: arises, rose, dawned |

| Psalm 19:6 | "The sun is on a circuit" | sur'-kit | Verb; to go around |
|---|---|---|---|
| Ecclesiastes 1:5 | "The sun rises, and the sun goes down" | zaw-rakh' and yaw-tsaw | Verbs: to come out |
| Psalm 104:19 | "The sun knows it's going down" | yarad | Verb: to descend |
| Psalm. 104:22 | "When the sun rises" | zaw-rakh' | Verb: arises, rose, dawned |
| Isaiah 60:20 | "Your sun shall no longer go down" | halak | Verb: to go, to come. |
| Job 9:7 | "He commands the sun and it does not rise" | zaw-rakh' | Verb: arises, rose, dawned |
| Joshua 10:12 | "Sun stand still!" | 1.qum 2. chashah | 1. Verb: to rise 2. Verb: to be inactive or still |
| Joshua 10:13 | "So the sun stood still and the moon stopped" | shabath | Verb; To cease, desist, rest |
| Habakkuk 3:11 | "The sun and the moon stood still in their habitation" | chashah | Verb; To be inactive or still |
| Leviticus 22:7 | "When the sun goes down" | Halak | Repeat |
| Deuteronomy 16:6 | "At the going down of the sun" | Halak | Repeat |
| Joshua 10:27 | "At the going down of the sun" | Halak | Repeat |
| Genesis 19:23 | "The sun had risen" | zarach | Verb; To rise, come forth. |
| Micah 3:6 | "The sun shall go down" | Halak | Repeat |
| Luke 4:40 | "When the sun was setting" | Yarad | Repeat |
| Ephesians 4:26 | "Don't let the sun go down on your wrath" | Halak | Repeat |
| James 1:11 | "The sun has risen" | Zarach | Repeat |

| Mark 16:2 | "When the sun had risen" | Zarach | Repeat |
|---|---|---|---|
| Exodus 17:12 | "The going down of the sun" | Halak | Repeat |
| Mark 1:32 | "When the sun had set" | Yarad | Repeat |
| Genesis 32:31 | "The sun was rising as Jacob left" | Zarach | Repeat |
| Exodus 14:27 | "So as the sun began to rise" | Zarach | Repeat |
| Psalm 65:8 | "The sun rises to where it sets" | Yarad | Repeat |
| Matthew 5:45 | "The sun rises on the just and the unjust" (Jesus) | Zarach | Repeat |
| Mark 4:6 | "But when the sun was up" | zaw-rakh' | Repeat |
| Joshua 12:1 | "Towards the rising of the sun" | Zarach | Repeat |
| Amos 8:9 | "I will make the sun go down" | Halak | Repeat |
| Jeremiah 15:9 | "Her sun has gone down" | Yarad | Repeat |
| Joshua 8:29 | "As soon as the sun was down" | Yarad | Repeat |
| Psalm 104:22 | "When the sun rises" | Zarach | Repeat |
| Psalm 50:1 | "From the rising of the sun to its going down" | zarach Halak | Repeat |
| 2 Chronicles 18:34 | "Sunset" | ereb | Noun or Verb (clarify): to sink, to settle |
| 1 Kings 22:36 | "As the sun was going down" | Halak | Repeat |
| 2 Samuel 23:4 | "When the sun rises" | Zarach | Repeat |

27

| 2 Samuel 2:24 | "The sun was going down" | Halak | Repeat |
|---|---|---|---|
| Judges 19:14 | "And the sun went down" | Halak | Repeat |
| Joshua 19:12 | "Toward the sunrise" | Zarach | Repeat |
| Judges 14:18 | "The seventh day before the sun went down" | Halak | Repeat |
| Joshua 19:27 | "Toward the sunrise" | Zarach | Repeat |
| Joshua 19:34 | "Toward the sunrise" | Zarach | Repeat |
| Deuteronomy 11:29 | "The setting sun" | Halak | Repeat |
| Exodus 22:3 | "If the sun has risen on him" | Zaw-rakh' | Repeat |
| Judges 9:33 | "As soon as the sun was up" | An-o' | Repeat |
| Joshua 1:15 | "The sunrising" | Za-rakh' | Repeat |
| Joshua 1:4 | "The going down of the sun" | Halak | Repeat |
| Isaiah 13:10 | "The sun will be dark when it rises" | zarach | Repeat |
| Judges 5:31 | "The sun comes out" | yaw-tsaw' | Verb: to come, pass, proceed, depart, came, went forth |

That's almost fifty more verses by various authors in the Old and New testament under the spirit-led voice of God clearly saying that the sun moves, and there are even more verses throughout other books in our Bible declaring that the sun moves. Many will argue that this was simply the perception of an ancient people, ignorant of the grandeur of space and our universe and galaxy that has been proven without a reasonable doubt, so don't doubt it, because if you do, you'll be labeled a danger to society, and we will ridicule you for these beliefs! It has been suggested that "context" is everything, and that all verses used need to be placed in their "proper context."

I contend that none of the verses used need any "context" at all. The sun moving was common knowledge, and God Himself clearly states that it moves. God never felt compelled to change the verbiage used because it was correct. Zero context needed. While I do not have a lengthy degree behind my name, I know what a metaphor is, and I know what a simile is. It is understood that when Jesus is called "the door of life," He is not an actual door. Moreover, God is not a bird, nor does He have feathers when the Word is giving an obvious metaphor of His attributes in Psalm 91.

These verses don't state that the sun is "like" anything; additionally, the verses clearly state the movement of the sun as nothing but fact.

If you believe the Bible is truly God's Word, you will concede to the argument that every single word was placed appropriately, used perfectly, and framed intelligently so as to relay the exact truths necessary to be saved and live in unity with God. God is not an author of confusion (*1 Corinthians 14:33*). He wants us to know the truth, and He has plainly laid it out in His Word. But this truth stands in complete contradiction with what we were taught and what most people think is true.

So now, how is it that a molten hot sun, supposedly ninety-three million miles away, shines its light through all darkness of space and ends up in our sky as a perfect circle of warmth, only to be blotted out by a small cloud and its heat taken away and no longer visible on a cloudy day? How does earth rotate around something that is that far away and the same force that causes it to do that, in gravity, also has the magic power of holding us down? Those are two very different functions associated from the same word. In the 2002, Henry Morris' book titled, *The Biblical Basis for Modern Science*, on page 228, he correctly states that "no one really understands gravity, or why it works as it does." It is my belief, based on common sense, that no one understands it because it's all a bunch of made-up hooey! If it can't be understood or demonstrated in a scientific experiment, then you can't use it as an explanation or scientific proof of anything.

The sun is not ninety-three million miles away like we were taught, God placed it in the firmament. If ninety-three million miles of dark vacuum cold space could not cool the sundown, how does a few little clouds accomplish such a magnificent feat on a wretchedly hot day? Let's face it, if we were a spinning planet, He would have shown us this in His Word. Would He not? It is His creation, and He clearly laid out a description of His sun and what it does in the Bible.

The sun, according to the Bible, moves. So then what of the earth?

Let's continue.

One verse that has been pointed out to me as a counter argument to my beliefs is *Isaiah 40:22*. And in some versions of the Bible (newer versions), it says, "He sits above the sphere of the earth" *Ah-ha!* There you have it, a sphere is a round ball. Not so fast. In the New King James and the King James, the wording says, "*He sits above the circle of the earth*," not a sphere, and a circle, is not a spinning ball, a sphere is three dimensional and a circle is not. Always stick with the closest known source of information. A few chapters back in the same book of *Isaiah 22:18*, it says, "*He will surely turn violently and toss you like a ball.*"

So you see, Isaiah could have used the Hebrew word meaning for ball in verse 22 to describe the shape of our earth, but he did not. That's because a ball is a ball and a circle is a circle. Some versions of the Bible, including the NIV and others, have committed a terrible sin in changing complete words with others because of how society may interpret it. Rather than us conforming to God's Word, we have tried to conform it to us. A very tactful move by the devil.

Why did this happen? Why this change? Perhaps to fit a narrative? An attempt to stay relevant perhaps? Whatever the reason, it violates a very serious warning from God in the book of Revelation.

> *For I testify unto every man that heareth the words of the prophecy of this book, If any man shall add unto these things, God shall add unto him the plagues that are written in this book:*
>
> *And if any man shall take away from the words of the book of this prophecy, God shall take away his*

*part out of the book of life, and out of the holy city,*
*and from the things which are written in this book.*
*(Revelation 22:18–19)*

Some will argue that these verses speak of only the book of Revelation. Possibly, then what? Can we feel free to change any verse in any book of the Bible that we want? Surely not, because Proverbs 30:6 in the Old Testament says *"Do not add to His words, lest He rebuke you, and you be found a liar"*

| Book and Verse | Emphasized Phraseology | Greek/ Hebrew | Definition |
|---|---|---|---|
| Job 22:14 | "He walks above the circle of heaven" | chug | Circle, circuit, compass |
| Proverbs 8:27 | "He drew a circle on the face of the deep" | "" | |
| Isaiah 40:22 | "He who sits above the circle of the earth" | "" | |

The Hebrew word for circle is a *noun*, meaning circle. This circle is a place—earth.

Our earth is indeed a circle, not a spinning ball, and the sun moves. This is what the Bible teaches. This is truth, and God got it right.

Let's consider these facts about the Word of God.

God, being all-knowing, tells in the Old Testament to His people, that the eighth day is the day when a baby boy should be circumcised. What's that got to do with anything you might wonder? Well, modern medicine only knew this being the most ideal day to perform this procedure due to vitamin K, which hardens the blood, being at its highest level on the eighth day of a baby boy's life. But God in His all-knowing wisdom tells the people over three thousand years ago that the eighth day is when it should be done (*Leviticus 12:3*).

If God could relay that kind of detailed medical information to His people to write in His Word, then surely, He could have whispered to the authors of His books that the sun indeed does not move and that we are the ones moving. Let's take a look to see what the Bible has to say about the earth and if us spinning around at one thousand miles per hour, as we've been taught, is true or not. We will look at the world's "evidence" in another chapter, but first let's go back to the scriptures and see what the Creator said about our "planet."

| Book and Verse | Emphasized Phraseology | Greek/Hebrew | Definition |
|---|---|---|---|
| 1 Samuel 2:8 | "The world is set on pillars | Maw-tsook | column |
| Job 9:6 | "The pillars tremble" | " | " |
| Psalm 75:3 | "The pillars are firm" | " | " |
| 1 Chronicles 16:30 | "The world shall not move" | koon | fixed |
| Psalm 96:10 | "The world shall not move" | " | " |
| Psalm 104:5 | "The foundations of the earth shall not be moved" | Mo-saw-daw | foundation |
| Psalm 93:1 | "The world cannot be moved" | repeat | |
| Isaiah 48:13 | "I laid the foundation of the earth" | repeat | |
| Matthew 13:34 | "The foundation of the world" | repeat | |
| Hebrews 1:10 | "He laid the foundation of the world" | repeat | |
| Hebrews 9:26 | "The foundation of the world" | repeat | |
| Hebrews 11:10 | "The city which has foundations whose builder and maker is God" | repeat | |
| Hebrews 4:3 | "The foundation of the world" | repeat | |
| 2 Timothy 2:19 | "The solid foundation of God stands" | repeat | |

| Peter 1:20 | "Before the foundation of the world" | repeat | |
|---|---|---|---|
| Revelation 21:14 | "The city had 12 foundations" | repeat | |
| Revelation 21:19 | "The foundation of the wall, the first foundation was Jasper" | repeat | |
| Luke 11:50 | "The foundation of the world" (Jesus) | repeat | |
| Ephesians 1:4 | "The foundation of the world" | repeat | |
| Job 26:11 | "The pillars that hold up the sky tremble" | ydwmu | pillars |
| Micah 6:2 | "Strong foundations of the earth" | repeat | |
| Psalm 24:2 | "for He laid the earths foundation on the seas and built it on the oceans depths" | repeat | |
| 2 Samuel 22:16 | "The foundations of the earth were exposed and seen" | repeat | |
| Matthew 12:42 | "The ends of the earth" | Per-as | End. Utmost part |
| Amos 9:6 | "the Lord's home reaches up to heaven while its foundation is on the earth: | repeat | |

Notice the word *planet* is never used. *Planet* is a made-up word; there is no such thing. He placed the sun and the moon and the stars in the firmament. That's all. A lot more to come on this ahead.

The Hebrew word for pillars is *Ydwmu*. Good luck pronouncing that one. It is the same word used in *Judges 16:25–26* to describe supports for a house and the pillars of the tabernacle in *Exodus 27:10–11*. Twenty-plus verses that say the world, our world, is immovable and set on a firm foundation with strong pillars holding it up. This is the Word of God.

Let's take a look at *Job 38*. God gives us descriptions of our world in many of the books of the Bible starting in Genesis, but here in Job, He describes the ends of the earth which is spoken about in many of the other books of the Bible.

This passage in *Job* reveals amazing insight of our world and how it was made. The Bible describes in detail what parts of our earth look like here. The setting is this: God is talking to Job and tells Job that He will ask the questions and Job will have to answer Him. God tells Job to prepare yourself like a man!

His first question to Job:

> Where were you when I laid the foundations of the earth?" (v.4)

> To what were its foundations fastened?" (v.6)

> Who laid its cornerstone?" (v.6)

> Where were you when I fixed my limit for it and set bars and doors? [speaking of the earth] (V.10)

> This far you may come but no further…and here your proud waves must stop. (v.11)

> Have you commanded the morning since your days began and caused the dawn to know its place? That it might take hold of the ends of the earth. (vv.12–13)

> Who has divided a channel for the overflowing of water? (v.25)

> The waters harden like stone and the surface of the deep is frozen. (v.30)

| Book and Verse | Emphasized Phraseology | Note |
|---|---|---|
| Luke 11:31 | "The ends of the earth" | Jesus speaking. "Ends" in Greek (peras) meaning "limit" |
| Acts 1:8 | "The ends of the earth" | Jesus speaking again. |
| Romans 10:18 | "Ends of the world" | There is no end on a ball. |
| Revelation 20:8 | "The four corners of the earth" | There are no corners on a ball. |
| Job 27:3 | "His lighting to the ends of the earth" | |
| Proverbs 30:4 | "Who established all the ends of the earth." | |
| Psalm 19:4 | "Their words went to the end of the world" | |
| Psalm 19:6 | "The sun rising from one end of heaven and its circuit to the other end" | |
| Micah 5:4 | "The ends of the earth" | |
| Isaiah 40:28 | "The Creator of the end of the earth" | |
| Matthew 12:42 | "She came from the ends of the earth" | |
| Jerimiah 16:19 | "Ends of the earth" | |
| Isaiah 11:12 | "Four corners of the earth" | |
| Revelation 7:1 | "Angels standing on the four corners of the earth" | |

Can we agree as born-again Christians that our Lord and Savior does not want us to be ignorant?

It looks like there is an end to our world, the Bible says so. But if all these verses are flowery, figuratively, not meant to be taken literal words, then the God of everything that we put all our trust in is then indeed a God of confusion, and the Bible has lied to us. How do we know what is literal or what is poetry? What is true and what is not? He has told us in these many verses that our sun moves and is in the firmament, that our earth does not move and has a sturdy foundation, and that there is an end to our world but that He has set limits as to how far we are allowed to go. He has set up channels so when the water overflows, it goes somewhere (answers the question about Noah and the flood as to where all the water went when the flood had passed), and there are indeed ice walls stopping our waves in the frozen deep.

*Job 38:25* says this: "*Who has divided a channel for the overflowing of water?*" Again in verse 30, "*The waters harden like stone.*" Again in chapter 38 verse 11, "*And here your proud waves must stop.*"

These verses are backed up by *Proverbs 8:27 and 29*—"*When He drew a circle on the face of the deep*" and "*when He assigned to the sea its limits.*"

"So, what's the big deal?"

"What difference does it make? Why all the fuss? This doesn't change anything about my salvation or how I live my life."

It makes all the difference in the world.

If we live in a protected environment, then someone (God) built it for us. We don't believe that a house or buildings just appear, do we? No. We assume that a carpenter and a plumber and an electrician and other trades came up with a plan and then executed that plan to build that structure. Say goodbye to the Big Bang theory and evolution too. Lies that are still taught as fact in our schools today. Try to mention a Creator in a college class and see what happens. Your GPA will suffer that much is certain.

Even as more and more of the science community has realized that we were indeed fearfully and wonderfully made by a "higher intelligence," the Big Bang theory and evolution and even aliens are still being pushed down our throats on a moment-by-moment basis in our schools of every level and media and film and TV. Think not? Think again.

Go find ten random people and do your own study. Take your own poll. Ask them if they believe in outer space and aliens and ETs. We are and have been brainwashed into far more than anyone may realize. It's just like Satan, as cunning as he is, to mix a little of God's truth in with his lies.

Two plus two is four, and the world is a round, spinning globe.

How do you think that our world ended up with all the false cult religions we have today? A little bit of truth and a whole lot of lies. The last book in the Bible, Revelation, gives a warning in its last verses of that book.

> *If anyone adds to these things, God will add to him the plagues that are written in this book, and if anyone takes away from the words of this book, God shall take away his part from the Book of Life.*

That is some serious stuff. God gave us His perfect Word and all other words that don't agree with the Bible are lies. The Lord God has shown us through His perfect Word the truth of His salvation plan to save this world from our sin. My heart breaks for those people who have fallen into Satan's false religions that he spawned to deceive us with.

# CHAPTER 3

# Space and the Moon

*Then God made two great lights, the greater to rule the day and the lesser to rule the night.*

*—Genesis 1:16*

First off, Satan is a liar. The Bible calls him the father of lies (*John 8:44*). A pretty good title for him. When we are first introduced to him in chapter 3 of Genesis, the first words out of his mouth are lies that cost us humans dearly. The world is his, and he travels back and forth (note: not around), seeking whom he may devour (*1 Peter 5:8*).

He has his grip on this world and takes everything good God has given to us and turns it into lies. Take Hollywood for example and the filth that has been put to film. Sex is a wonderful amazing gift from God, and Satan has turned it into perversion. The porn industry is one of the biggest industries of all time. Food has become obsession when it was meant for fuel. Singing was meant to praise God, and now it's filth to describe women and men engaging is heinous acts and to hate authority.

Satan has even highjacked Christmas with Santa, a palindrome for Satan. Not so subtle of a twist from the devil with that one, and yet hidden in plain sight. Think about it, Jesus's birth celebration taken over by a god-like figure that knows when you are sleeping and knows when you're awake and if you've been good or bad and rewards you, and we leave an offering to him of cookies and milk. It used to be wine and fruitcakes that were left, meant to curry favor.

A child is told this, sings songs about him, waits and prays that they will get what they want, and then finds out that this "god" is not real at another tender age. What do you think the chances are that this same child will come to believe in the true and real God when they get older? Santa-god is pushed on us with songs and movies and children's books almost as much as something else—the globe, a stationary sun, and space!

Watch your television for a day and notice how many times the globe is pushed in our faces. It's in almost every movie, sitcoms, and advertisements. Heck, it's the Universal Studios logo. The NFL uses it, all the news stations use it. We have had "pictures" shoved in our face of a round spinning globe for our entire life and around the clock, 24/7/365.

In 1977, I was twelve years old. My Dodgers were playing well and making a run at the world series. I wasn't an adult and was not aware of the strife happening in our country. The economy was sluggish, the Son of Sam was terrorizing New York, and I do remember hearing about the blackouts in New York with the widespread crime, looting and panic amidst a bad heat wave. But in Southern California, life was pretty easy. I think that my parents' only concern were the gas lines and what to do with their high-energy kid (me). The beach was free, and movies were cheap, so we spent a lot of time at the beach and at the movies. My little brother was really into space movies, and *Star Wars* had just come out in the theaters.

I remember taking him to see it. He was clutching Darth Vader and Luke Skywalker action figurines in his hands and was very excited. Movies have never been my thing, and I was probably annoyed at having to keep an eye on him even if it meant a free trip to the show. I have to admit that I liked the movie, but not like my brother and other people. There was a grown adult at my church that told me he saw the movie over forty times! Mind you, there were no Blockbusters, no VHS, no DVDs, and certainly nothing streaming at this time. Cable was just coming out, and we had five TV stations.

Even at $4.50 a ticket, this guy invested $180 back in 1977 to watch the same thing over and over again. People were going to the show dressing up as the characters in the movie, and my brothers' toys were a hot commodity, it was a world wide phenomena.

*Star Wars* was everywhere. It still is.

It struck me as weird then, and it still does today now, with the tenth or eleventh movie coming out. None of it was real, just science fiction, but people ate it up. The premise of the movie is classic good versus evil. It was gold then and gold still to this day. The second one was good too. After that, I was in high school and all the madness that comes with it took over my social life and any interest in movies was gone. A lot of things have changed since then. We have thousands of channels on our televisions. We have cellphones and the internet that has so much information at our fingertips that it's scary to think about. There is no need to go to a library or own a set of encyclopedias like we had to back in the day, just type or talk into your phone and every bit of useful and useless information is available. Today we live in science fiction.

Social media drives part of our economy and the influences of platforms like Instagram, Facebook, Snapchat, and others dominate our youth. Movies and television are and always have been influential and Satan knows this. People want to escape, be entertained, forget reality for a while, or take a nap. Problem is that what goes through our eyes and into our minds is programming us, just like the globe and Santa of our youth. YouTube videos and Instagram provide constant programming of our minds.

Do you think that we aren't being programmed?

Here is an incomplete list of movies that have been brainwashing the masses since film came into our lives. Look at this list and you decide if there is a concentrated effort to get us to believe in something that's not real.

Space/alien movies are the most made movies of all time, it's not even close.

| Flash Gordan | Lost in Space | War of the Worlds | It Came from Outer Space (1953) | A Trip to Mars (1918) |
|---|---|---|---|---|
| A Son of Mars (1912) | A Message from Mars (1921) | The Man from Mars (1922) | Aelita (1924) | Vamping Venus (1928) |
| Just Imagine (1928) | Teenagers from Outer Space (1959) | Zontar: the Thing from Venus (1966) | Mars Attacks the World (1938) | Rocket to Mars (1946) |
| Boom in the Moon (1946) | Rocketship X-M (1950) | Red Planet Mars (1952) | Flight to Mars (1951) | The Day the Earth Stood Still (1951) |
| Termites from Mars (1952) | Invaders from Mars (1953) | Abbott and Costello Go to Mars (1953) | Phantom from Space (1953) | Spaceways (1953) |
| Duck Dodgers in the 24 1/2th Century (1953) | Killers from Space (1954) | Project Moonbase (1953) | Popeye, the Ace of Space (1953) | Beyond the Moon (1954) |
| Devil Girl from Mars (1954) | Crash of the Moons (1954) | Conquest of Space (1955) | Music from Mars (1955) | Plan 9 from Outer Space |
| Queen of Outer Space (1958) | Close Encounters of the Third Kind (1977) | ET (1982) | Star Wars (1977) | Star Wars 2 |
| Star Wars 3 | Star Wars 4 | Star Wars 5 | Star Wars 6 | Star Wars 7 |
| Star Wars 8 | Star Wars 9 | Star Wars 10 | Star Wars 11 | Rogue One |
| Star Wars cartoons | Battle Star Galatica | Star Trek 1966 | Star Trek Deep Space 9 | Star Trek Voyager |
| Star Trek TNG | Star Trek Discovery | Star Trek Enterprise | Star Trek cartoons | Star Trek Picard |
| The Oriville | The Outer Limits | The Twilight Zone | The Jetsons | Dark Matter |
| Bitten | First Wave | Killjoys | Firefly | The Expanse |
| Stargate Atlantis | Stargate SG 1 | Farscape Babylon 5 | Star Trek Discovery | Andromeda |
| The 100 | Red dwarf | Space: Above and Beyond | Eureka | Flash Gordan (1980) |

| | | | | |
|---|---|---|---|---|
| Starcrash (1978) | Abraxas, Guardian of the Universe (1990) | Iron Sky (2012) | Leprechaun in Space (1997) | Laserblast (1978) |
| Transmorphers (2007) | Barbarella (1968) | Time Walker (1982) | Battle Beyond the Stars (1980) | Space Hunters (1983) |
| 2001 Space Odyssey (1968) | 2001 A Space Travesty (2000) | Galaxina (1980) | Space Mutiny (1988) | Alien (1979) |
| Aliens (1986) | Alien 3 (1992) | Alien Resurrection (1997) | Prometheus (2012) | Alien Covenant (2017) |
| Alien vs. Hunter (2007) | Alien vs. Predator (2004) | Alien vs. Predator 2 (2007) | Alien vs. Predator 3 (2010) | Invasion of the Body Snatchers (1956) |
| Invasion of the Body Snatchers (1978) | Cat Women of the Moon (1953) | Robot Monster (1953) | Monster a Go Go (1965) | Santa Conquers the Martians (1964) |
| 1st Contact | Mission to Mars | Rocky Horror Picture Show | Space (1999) | Space Age (1992) |
| Dr. Who | Interstellar (2014) | First Man (2018) | Ad Astra (2019) | Alf |
| The Right Stuff | The Martian (2015) | Independence Day (1996) | Serenity (2005) | John Carter (2012) |
| Apollo 13 (1995) | Dune (1984) | Armageddon (1998) | Stargate (1994) | Galaxy Quest (1999) |
| Hitchhikers Guide to the Galaxy (2005) | A Wrinkle in Time (2018) | Superman 1 | Superman 2 | Superman 3 |
| Superman vs Batman | Man of Steel | Fantastic 4 (2005) | Independence Day: Resurgence (2016) | Men in black 1 |
| Men in Black 2 | Men in Black 3 (2012) | Tomorrowland (2015) | Contact (1997) | Pitch Black (2000) |
| Total Recall (1990) | Event Horizon (1997) | Space Balls (1987) | Space Jam (1996) | Oblivion (2013) |

| | | | | |
|---|---|---|---|---|
| Moonraker 1979 | Planet of the apes 1 | Planet of the apes 2 | Planet of the apes 3 | Planet of the apes 4 |
| Planet of the Apes 5 | Jason in Space | Lucy in the Sky | Porxima | Valerian and the City of a Thousand Planets |
| Passengers | Europa report | Oct Sky (1999) | Hidden Figures (2017) | Wall-e (2008) |
| The Abyss (1989) | The Alpha Incident (1977) | Android (1982) | Arena (1989) | The Arrival (1996) |
| The Arrival 2 (1988) | The Atomic Sub (1959) | Bad Taste (1987) | Bad Channels (1992) | The Beast with One Million Eyes |
| Bad Moon Risen (1988) | Black Hole (1979) | The Brain from Planet Arous (1958) | A Brother from Another Planet (1984) | Buck Rogers (1939) |
| Buck Rogers in the 25th Century (1979) | Capricorn One (1978) (surprised that this film was actually made) | The Cat from Outer Space (1978) | Cocoon (1985) | Cocoon Return (1988) |
| Tom Corbit, Space Cadet (1950) | The Cosmic Man (1972) | Creature (1985) | The Creeping Terror (1964) | Daleks Invasion Earth (1966) |
| Dark City (1998) | Dark Side of the Moon (1989) | Dark Star (1974) | Day of Triffids (1963) | The Day the Earth Caught Fire (1962) |
| Deadly Ray from Mars (1938) | Deep Impact (1998) | Deep Star Six (1989) | Disney Ducktales Space Invaders (1990) | Dog Star Man (1964) |
| Earth vs. the Flying Saucer (1957) | Enemy Mine (1985) | Explores (1985) | Eyes Behind the Stars (1972) | Fantastic Planet (1973) |
| Fire in the Sky (1993) | First Man into Space (1958) | First Man in the Moon (1964) | First Spaceship on Venus (1960) | The Fifth Element (1997) |

| | | | | |
|---|---|---|---|---|
| Flight of the Navigator (1986) | Flight to Mars (1951) | The Flying Saucer (1950) | Forbidden Planet (1956) | From Earth to the Moon (1958) |
| Galaxina (1980) | Galaxy of Terror (1981) | The Gifted (1993) | The Green Slime (1969) | The Groundstar Conspiracy (1972) |
| Hanger 18 (1980) | The Hidden (1987) | Horror of the Blood Monster (1970) | Hyper Sapien (1986) | I Come in Peace (1990) |
| I Married a Monster from Outer Space (1958) | I Was a Zombie for the FBI (1982) | Ice Pirates (1984) | The Incredible Melting Man (1978) | Intruders (1992) |
| Invader (1991) | The Invaders (1995) | Invasion of the Animal People (1962) | Invasion of the Bee Girls (1973) | Invasion Earth (1987) |
| Invasion of the Neptune Men (1967) | Invasion UFO (1980) | It Conquered the World (1956) | Terror from Beyond Space (1958) | Journey to the Far-Side of the Sun (1969) |
| Jungle Hell (1955) | Killers from Space (1954) | Outpost Zeta (1980) | Kronos (1957) | Laboratory (1980) |
| Last Star Fighter (1984) | Lifeforce (1985) | Lifepod 1978 | Lifepod Remake (1993) | The Lost Planet (1953) |
| Mac and Me (1988) | The Man Who Fell to Earth (1976) | Marooned (1969) | Mars Attacks (1996) | Mars Needs Women (1966) |
| The Martian Chronicles (1979) | Master of Venus | Men into Space (1959) | Metamorphosis (1993) | Meteor (1979) |
| Missile to the Moon (1958) | The Cyclon Attack (1979) | Mission Mars (1968) | Mission Stardust (1968) | Moon 44 (1990) |
| Moon Trap (1989) | Muppets from Space (1999) | Murder by Moonlight (1989) | Murder in Space (1985) | The Mysterians (1959) |
| Mysterious Planet (1984) | Night of the Comet (1984) | Nightfall (1988) | Not of This Earth (1988) | Night-Flyers (1987) |

| | | | | |
|---|---|---|---|---|
| Nukie (1993) | Official Denial (1993) | The Omega Imperative (1968) | Outbreak (1995) | Outland (1981) |
| Pajama Party (1964) | Peacemaker (1990) | The People (1971) | Phantom Empire (1935) | Phantom Planet (1961) |
| Phantom from Space (1953) | Phoenix (1995) | Planet of Blood (1966) | Planet of the Dinosaurs (1978) | Planet on the Prowl (1965) |
| Planets Against Us (1961) | Predator 1 (1987) | Predator 2 (1990) | Prince of Space (1959) | Prisoner of the Lost Universe (1983) |
| Project Alien (1990) | Project Genesis (1993) | Project Moon Base (1953) | Psi Factor | The Puppet Master (1994) |
| The Quatermass Experiment (1956) | The Quatermass Experiment 2 (1957) | Quiet Earth (1985) | Radar Men from the Moon (1952) | Raygun Justice (1979) |
| Return of Aliens (1983) | Robinson Crusoe on Mars (1964) (No, I didn't make that one up.) | Rocketship (1936) | Rocky Jones, Space Ranger (1954) | Roswell UFO Coverup (1994) |
| Satans Satellites (1952) | Saturn 3 (1980) | The Silencers (1995) | Silent Running (1971) | Solar Crisis (1993) |
| Solar Force (1994) | Solarbabies Invasion USA | Riders to the Stars 1954 | Space Mutiny (1988) | The Thing |
| Lost Continent | Invasion USA | Them (1954) | Gog (1954) | Target Earth (1954) |
| Stranger from Venus (1954) | This Is Island Earth (1955) | Timeslip (1955) | Creature with the Atom Brain (1955) | The Gamma People (1956) |
| Fire Maiden From Space | 20 Million Miles to Earth (1957) | The 27th Day (1957) | The Cyclops (1957) | Planet X |

| Space Children 1958 | Space master | The Blob (1958) Cosmic Man (1959) | Stranger Things (2018) | Mork and Mindy |
|---|---|---|---|---|
| My Favorite Martian | Lost in Space (remake 2019–2020) | War of the Worlds remake (Netflix) | | |

"It is easier to fool people than to convince them that they've been fooled" (Mark Twain).

That is a long list, and the sheer number of movies listed proves that space/alien movies are quite the money-maker for Hollywood. Wonder why?—This is a concentrated effort to brainwash us with fantasy and lies to control and influence our thoughts. There are a lot more, and we barely touched the television shows about space and didn't even mention the hundreds of books and radio shows.

Just imagine another four pages of bad space and alien movies that you'd never want to see anyway.

This is pure propaganda disguised as entertainment. The *War of the Worlds* that was mentioned at the top of the list is a great example of being able to lead and fool the masses. It was 1938 when Orson Wells took to the airwaves on public radio and caused widespread panic. People actually thought that we were being invaded by Martians because of his reading of a fictional book. Paul warns of this in *Colossians 2:8*, "*Beware lest anyone cheat you through philosophy and empty deceit, according to the basic principles of the world, and not according to Christ.*" How did your poll turn out? A lot more people believe in aliens than you thought, right? It's no wonder.

Here's a follow up question for your poll. Ask the same ten people if they believe in God. Satan knows an easy target when he sees it. It has been said that the devil's best scheme to lull you into his will is that he tries to make you not believe in him, that he's just a silly red cartoon character not to be taken seriously. Kind of like Santa, but unlike Santa, Satan is real, and he's real interested in taking you with him into a pit of fire for all eternity.

Confession, I've only seen a handful of the movies listed, but movies about space are basically all the same, and it was an easy

Google search to find a lot of space and alien movies. After reading the descriptions of most all the listed movies; it is obvious that we were really into Mars back in the '50s. With a programmed population watching all those movies in the 1950s and '60s, it was an easy sell that man would soon be walking on the moon. President Kennedy said many times in many speeches that we would put a man on the moon, and he even gave a time frame that made it seem more legitimate and feasible.

Oh no, not a moon denial guy too? Yep, think about it, where is space in the firmament? *Star Wars* looked a heck of a lot more real than any film footage or "real" pictures we have today, even back in 1977. We only have bad grainy film of those supposed moon landings. We have more technology in our cellphones of ten years ago than the "astronauts" had on their "spacecraft" in the late '60s and early '70s.

Oh, we make fine rockets, but we have never put a man on the moon. There are so many holes in the "fake moon landings" that the topic alone should be a book of its own. Our "astronauts" were compromised. Saying this out loud gets people really riled up. But people can tell the difference between bad CGI and good CGI today. Regardless, it's all CGI, and back then it wasn't even CGI, it was early photoshop and the filmmaking easily shows the flaws of the era in which the films were made. Moreover, the people in charge of duping us all could not think of everything, and it shows. The footage and pictures we see on an almost daily basis are obviously fake.

There is a news app on my cellphone, and almost every day there are short columns written about something in space, complete with more fake pictures that are clearly fake even from viewing on my little phone screen. These pictures and stories are not even meant to be read. You're just supposed to scroll by them and have them enter into your mind; this creates a subliminal message that reinforces what you've been taught. Look for a moment and swipe right. Once you break through the programming, you see the obvious methods being used by the world to control you and what you believe reality to be.

NASA spots WHAT?

Should 'X-files' be made public?

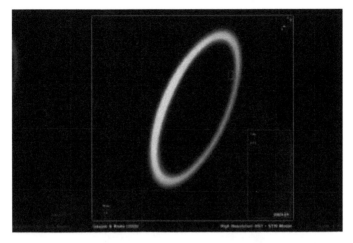

# 'Disappearing' exoplanet may have never existed, scientists believe

# Alien planet is so hot it's tearing itself apart

When Googling the word *planets*, this is what came up under images. Please be honest with yourself, does this look real to you? Why does NASA put out such blatantly fake photos if this is fact? Where's the legitimacy?

These are artists making it up. Go ahead and Google more pictures of these same planets and see if one Saturn looks like the next as seen above. For that matter, Google pictures of earth and see if they look like other pictures of earth.

Our "astronauts" were actor-onauts.

Let's ask a hypothetical question. If you knew classified information and you were told that if you ever told anyone, your family would suffer, your kids would suffer, and your grandkids would suffer, what would you do? When there is an agenda that has to be sold, those at the top can and will do anything. I don't believe everything on the video platform YouTube, but there is a lot of footage of former "astronauts" acting in crazy ways and saying lots of crazy stuff. Look them up for yourself. Start with Buzz Aldrin. Buzz Aldrin (the 2nd man to walk on the moon) has been video recorded saying that we did not go to the moon. He is an old man now and maybe not seen as a threat anymore but can we believe him? It has been hypothesized with a lot of evidence that men were killed in "accidents" surrounding the space program due to their lack of cooperation, sending a clear message to the others to toe the line. And even if we did the astronomical event, then why don't we celebrate the "moon-landing" every year like other major holidays? Shouldn't this have been a date to remember. Here is another picture that is really hard to believe.

This is a picture of our thirty-seventh President Richard Nixon on a landline phone call in 1972 talking to astronauts on the moon 250,000 miles away. Use common sense here. Is it necessary to comment further? the picture speaks for itself. Think about the technology we did not have back in 1972. We don't have cellphones today that could reach 250,000 miles. Seriously? We need cellphone towers today every few miles or so here on earth. You've seen them, sometimes they try to hide them by blending them in with trees. So just where are the cellphone towers between earth and the 250,000 miles to the moon, and what other propaganda have we bought into? This was elaborate, this was intentional, this is deception at the highest level, and it has all been lies. It is clear that "they" never thought that the human population would have at its fingertips the kind of technology that we do indeed have today, and it's right in the palm of our hands. But what silly things do we do with this amazing technology? We take selfies and watch cat videos.

Satan is indeed the most cunning trickster, what wouldn't he attempt to manipulate us with? As soon as the internet was available to the population, lies and envy and porn dominated it. Today most everyone has a cellphone and a computer or access to them, and what dominates on them? We are distracted by the crap on the phones and pay attention to little else. Okay then, what does the Bible say about the moon? The only other "planet" we've never been to.

| Book and Verse | Emphasized Phraseology | Notes |
|---|---|---|
| Deuteronomy 17:3 | "bowing to worship the sun, moon, and stars I have forbidden." | |
| Ezekiel 32:7 | "The moon will not give its light" | Does not need the sun |
| Matthew 24:29 | "The moon gives its own light" | "" |
| Isaiah 1:14 | "I hate your new moon party" | |
| Job 31:26 | "The moon is moving" | |
| Isaiah 13:10 | "The moon is its own light" | "" |
| Deuteronomy 4:19 | "When you look to the heavens and see the sun, moon, and stars, do not be led astray to bow in worship to them and serve them." | Note, no planets |
| 1 Samuel 20:18 | "Tomorrow is a new moon." | |

| | | |
|---|---|---|
| 1 Samuel 20:24 | "At the new moon, the king sat to eat the meal" | |
| 1 Samuel 20:34 | "Angry, He did not eat any food that 2nd day of the new moon." | |
| 2 Kings 23:5 | "They had burned incense to Baal, and to the sun, moon, constellations, and all the stars in the sky" | Note, no planets |
| 2 Kings 4:23 | "It is not a new moon or the Sabbath" | |
| Nehemiah 10:33 | "A new moon offering" | |
| Job 25:5 | "Even if the moon does not shine." | Because it does |
| Psalm 8:3 | "I observe your heavens, the work of your fingers, the moon and the stars, which you set in place." | Again, no planets |
| Psalm 74:16 | "The day is yours, also the night, you established the moon and the sun" | And no planets |
| Psalm 81:3 | "Feast during the new moon and during the new moon." | |
| Psalm 104:19 | "He made the moon to mark the festivals, the sun knows when to set." | The sun moves |
| Psalm 89:37 | "Like the moon, established forever, a faithful witness in the sky" | |
| Psalm 136:9 | "The moon and stars to rule by night" | |
| Proverbs 7:20 | "He will come home at the time of the full moon" | |
| Isaiah 66:23 | "All mankind will come to worship me from one new moon to another" | |
| Ezekiel 32:7 | "The moon will not give its light" | |
| Ezekiel 46:1 | "On the day of the new moon" | |
| Ezekiel 46:6 | "On the day of the new moon" | |
| Hosea 5:7 | "The new moon" | |
| Joel 2:31 | "The sun will be turned into darkness and the moon to blood before the Great and terrible day of the Lord comes" | |

| Amos 8:5 | "When will the new moon be over?" | |
| --- | --- | --- |
| Mark 13:24 | "The moon will not shed its light" | |
| 1 Corinthians 15:41 | "There is a splendor of the sun, another of the moon, and another for the stars, in fact, one star differs from another star in splendor" | No planets |
| Colossians 2:16 | "A new moon" | |
| Revelation 21:23 | "The city does not need the sun or the moon to shine on it, because the Glory of God illuminates it" | Let there be light |

So the moon is a clock and a light, filling up and emptying out. It was made for seasons. It is its own light, separate from the sun, not needing to reflect the sun's light (like we were taught), and we are commanded not to worship the sun or the moon. Consider this fact: during a full lunar eclipse, how does the moon produce a glow from behind the shadow? The sun is not causing the glow because the shadow in front of the moon won't allow it. Therefore, the moon produces its own light. As a Christian, placing a non-moving sun as the center of our "universe" is a form of sun worship. It makes the sun more special than earth where God's image (us) were placed to rule over all His other creations. All the planetary pictures and "theories" of how our system works are blatant lies or God is lying. The earth is just as it is described in the Bible. It is time that the lid be blown off of this madness. Trust your senses, trust science, trust God's natural laws.

Time for some science (which God created)

There is a tool called a temperature gun. It is used to gauge the temperature of any surface area. It will cost you less than $20 at your local hardware store or online. Point it at any surface that you wish, and it will read the temperature of that surface. Go outside on a sunny day and read the degree of heat on the ground in full sun. Then read the degree of heat on the same ground that has the shade of a tree or building on it. The shaded area will be cooler. Makes sense? Yes.

Now take your new tool outside at night. Do the same experiment and read the ground temperature in the moonlight and then compare it with a ground reading of an area that the moonlight is not touching. What happens? If you didn't do it, the results are amazing! The moonlight that doesn't have a shadow blocking it is actually cooler than the area with no moonlight (roughly twelve degrees cooler in fact). The moon gives off its own cooler light and is not a reflection of the sun.

Another fun fact about our moon is this. No one has ever seen the other side of the moon. Forget the movies and what you've been told by systems of government. The moon rolls through the sky every night. This is observed by simply watching it. There are markings on the moon referred to as the "rabbit in the moon" because it resembles a curled-up bunny with its ears showing. These markings make it easy to witness the rolling motion of the moon. Test this. Go outside and snap a picture of the moon and have a buddy in another state or even better, another country, do the same thing. Have them send their picture to you and you send yours to them. There will be the same markings of the moon in your picture and your friends' picture because no one has ever seen even a quarter inch of the "backside" of our moon. From Los Angeles to Russia to Japan and Africa, we all see the same face of the moon and never the back. The only time anyone has ever "seen" the dark side of the moon was in a fake Hollywood movie or maybe on their own personal acid trip.

Everyone has seen this as well. Go outside on a clear day. The sun is up, and the moon is out. The moon is only a half-moon today, and instead of a shadow or an outline, you can see a pretty sky blue through the moon, and also the "shadow" the earth is supposed to be making is on the wrong side. If the earth was in the way of the moon blocked by the sun, then how are both visible?

According to what we were taught in school, shouldn't we see the darkness of space through the moon instead of blue sky? Or at the very least an edge? And why is the moon see-through? Didn't we stand on it? In all the pictures from NASA, the stars are usually missing as well, and where did the glow of the moon go?

Here's another picture of a USA "spacecraft" leaving the moon on its way back to earth. One big question to ask here is "Who stayed behind on the moon to take the picture?" Are they still there? And again, where are the stars and the sun? The intense glow of the moon would likely make taking a picture an impossibility. How dumb do they think we are?

While trying to stick to the Bible for these questions and answers as much as possible, we need to avoid getting lost in the weeds on this topic and the topics coming up, but some of "the evidence" is just common sense, so here is a list of somethings to consider about the "moon landings."

1.   Science says that the earth spins at a thousand-plus miles an hour and that our atmosphere spins with us. At some point, the spinning must stop, and a spaceship would exit into the black still vacuum of space. No more spinning, right? Makes sense. So leaving something that is spinning into something that is not spinning would be like sticking

your finger into a spinning fan that's moving at a thousand miles per hour. Try that and see what happens. The spaceship would fair no better than your finger.

2. NASA (Never A Straight Answer) does what? Why do they get over thirty billion dollars a year from US taxpayers? This money, our money, is being used to promote the propaganda with all sorts of fake news about "space." It defies our common sense when our TV stations show footage from our "space station." It's the same every time—the microphone is floated from person to person and one of the "astronauts" will inevitably do a flip to prove that they are in zero gravity. None of it looks real and sometimes you can see the wires they are using to try and fool us; it defies the senses, and it's just bad filmography. Also has anyone noticed that the astronauts are always young and good looking? This helps sell the farce. Oh, and we are supposed to believe that there is a Tesla floating out there too. YouTube video of the Elon Musk rockets landing back on earth on their tails—talk about bad CGI. The government started this, and it has gone on for so long that it is accepted normal. To change one's way of thinking will cause the population to examine other issues as well and that scares the hell out of the players that are on top. If the government was in on this and it ever got legs out among the masses, it would be chaos! If it means knowing that the truth of God's Word would be made clear to all, some chaos is worth it! We don't need to hide from our senses anymore because rest assured that once the line has been crossed, it will change the way we look at everything.

3. Here is a "famous" picture of our earth taken from the moon. Have you seen this one? It's accepted; most everyone has seen it. Take a closer look with adobe photoshop, and you'll see that it has been photoshopped! More lies.

OFFICIAL NASA IMAGE SHOWING
THE "EARTH RISE" FROM THE MOON

ELEVATED EXPOSURE IN
PHOTOSHOP REVEALS
A COPY/PASTE JOB

4.  Another accepted picture of our culture is titled the "Blue marble" circa mid-1970s. This is our spinning earth, but alas, it too is a photoshopped artist image and not real. You'll notice the cloud patterns have been highlighted. The cloud patterns highlighted are identical, and science tells us that nothing in nature is identical, very snowflake is different than the next, every leaf on a tree is unique, and every face of a human is its own. Take a closer look at this "real picture from space" and answer this question. How is it that every continent is visible in broad daylight? It's dark in New York at 9pm when it is still light in California at 6pm, but in this picture from "space" it is light in Asia and Africa and Russia and the USA at the same time. There is no other explanation than this is another fake picture that was passed off as real and put on the cover of major magazines. If you have an iPhone, your default screensaver is this picture. Interesting.

5. The lie of the glow—where is the glow? The moon is its own light as told to us in the Bible, so where is the glow in any of the moon film footage or pictures? The glow is so bright here on earth that it can hurt your eyes staring at it for too long on certain nights. The intensity must be incredible two hundred fifty thousand miles closer. But it's not there in any film or pictures. We have been taught that our moon is two hundred fifty thousand miles away. We have also been taught that our highest clouds are around fifty-five miles up. I have seen with my own eyes clouds behind the moon. You have too. It just doesn't dawn on us to think about it. There is real film footage and real pictures of this.

The sun and moon are in our firmament.

There are many more issues surrounding our space program. A major factor in saying that we went to the moon was to put military and economic pressure on the old Soviet Union during the height of the Cold War. It was brilliant actually. Say that we are going to put man on the moon and then make it look like we did. Many cosmonauts from Russia died in attempts to reach "outer space." Very tragic in what they did, trying to keep up with the American lie.

Please forgive my asking you to Google and YouTube things, but this is the age we live in now, so please pull up Bill Nye "the science guy" and listen to him explain that we live in a "closed system" and that "we cannot leave earth's atmosphere."

People trust this guy and believe what he says because well, he's the science guy. Sad truth—he's not even a real scientist. Do you believe what he said about our closed system? Even a blind squirrel finds a nut now and then.

Meanwhile back on earth, there are basic principles at work here on our earth that we call science. God created science and put all the materials here on earth that we would need to create all the things that we have and enjoy and rely on today. If you live in a warm state, then you rely on your air conditioner. If you live in a cold state, then a good working heater is a must. We depend on these modern conveniences daily but never think, where did all the materials come from to make such wonderful and necessary machines? We can travel in cars, planes, trains, and ships because we found all the material we needed on and under our earth to make these things. God put them here for us. For most of our history here on earth, the fastest mode of transportation was a horse. We don't live in that day anymore, and we need to act like it. This is a terrible lie brought from the pits of hell and the human race has bought into it and the Christian church stands idly by while lies program our people. The USA is now showboating a new military branch called "Space Force" and the logo looks an awful lot like *Star Trek*. So invested in a lie that they are forced to keep adding to it and using television and movie imagery that people will recognize in order to make it seem more legitimate.

# CHAPTER 4

## Magic, Water, and Science

*And God made a wind to pass over the earth, and the waters subsided.*

—*Genesis 8:1*

After space and alien movies, the next most made movies are about fantasy and magic. Kids are enthralled with "magic" and always have been. I wanted to be a magician when I was young too, and Harry Potter wasn't even born yet. I remember getting my own little set of magic tricks at the Disneyland Magic store on main street, begging my mother until it was mine, not merely satisfied with a trip to Disneyland. Spoiled brat. I took it home and read the instructions and after too many failed attempts finally realized that it just wasn't in the cards for me. I was terrible and I had wasted my mother's money.

But what is magic? Deception is what it is! Sleight of hand look this way, while the deception is done that way. Speed, however, is not deceptive, we know when we are going fast. It matters not how large the vehicle is that is speeding you along your way, you will feel the movement. When you're in a fast-moving car, you know it; when you're flying in a plane, you can feel that it is moving much faster than the air around it. If the earth was a round, spinning ball moving at a thousand-plus miles per hour, we would feel it. I surely felt the speed of the roller-coaster on Space Mountain.

We do live in a magical world. The sun moves, the earth does not, the stars rotate but keep their patterns; however, the north star does not move. It is true and constant. This is a scientific fact, and it's magical. We can go outside each night and find the north star, and it does not matter where you live on this earth. It is always visible to everyone in every country come night time. This is not possible on a round earth. On a round, spinning earth, the north star would naturally be hidden at certain times. On a round, spinning earth, the north star would only always be visible in the North Pole at all times. If the earth moves, then the constellations would always look different. The human eye would see those constellations from different angles. But that is not what we see.

*First Corinthians 15:41* says this, "*There is one glory for the sun, another glory for the moon, and another glory of the stars, for one star differs from another star in glory.*" The moon does not need to reflect the sun's light, it has its own as do the stars, and all the stars are different from one another. Why wouldn't they be different? God made everything in nature different, it's easy for Him. Planets are not real, but the sun and the moon and the stars are. And one of those stars does not move. Our earth doesn't move, and Polaris, the brightest of all the stars does not move. The sun moves, the moon moves, and the stars move. The earth and one fixed star do not. *Deuteronomy 4:19* says,

> *Take heed lest you lift your eyes to heaven, and you see the sun, the moon, and the stars, all the host of heaven, don't feel driven to worship them and serve them.*

No man-made planets or science fiction, just real science, and our Creator made it all just the way He said He did.

Below are some more actual fake news blurbs that are captured on an almost daily basis on my cellphone. The pictures are obviously fake, and the news captions are laughable. Some even give dates as to the end of our world. Upon reading some of the articles, it is my opinion that they really are not meant to be read. Just swipe right and onto the next image. But the damage is done, isn't it? We saw the fake news blurb about something in space and a picture to go with it, and it entered our mind whether we realized it or not. Subliminal messaging is an old trick, and it works. This is yet another case of indoctrination. Put something in the face of people every day so it seems normal and accepted and soon it becomes just that and no one questions anything. Just the way the devil wants it. Mix lies and truth together, and soon no one will be able to tell the difference between the two. God's Word is the only truth that we can count on.

**In a first, space station astronaut's blood clot treated by doctors on Earth**

**Jupiter is flinging asteroids at Earth 'like a sniper', top scientist warns**

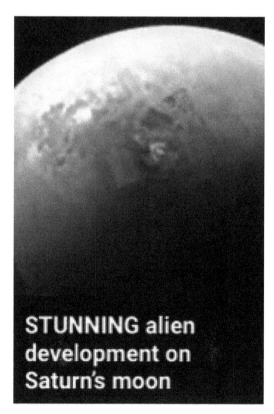

STUNNING alien development on Saturn's moon

Are there any converts in the house yet? Seriously, have you been challenged by the Word of God? There is no fear of anyone trying to challenge the truthfulness of these words because all that's basically been done here is to use God's own words to lay out the truth. If God is wrong, and there are indeed errors in the Bible, then we should know about that. But if God wrote what He wanted the way He wanted to, then God is right. Are we so haughty in our own wisdom that we feel ok with refuting the Creator of all? This is not myself attempting to speak for God; rather, it is letting myself be used by God to expose this awful lie. Once we let go of what we think we know or thought we knew and open our minds and hearts up to the simple and obvious truths found in His Holy Word, then we have clear eyes that can see the truths right in front of our faces.

What is now needed is prominent pastors and respected men and women of God to be faithful to what they know to be true. I am not alone; I am just one who doesn't care one whiff what the world thinks of me. It's all about what the Savior of mankind thinks.

Writing this book has been tough, I've been unable to share with friends and family all the truths that have been discovered. My wife and son are the exception, they have let me talk their ears off and allowed me to use them as an outlet and as a barometer as to how Christians will receive these revelations. Keeping it under wraps is understandable I feel as God Himself would have received pushback from humans if we were around to watch Him create the world. Look what we are doing now. You, along with most of the world, are believing that He made the sun something it's not and the same for the earth. "No, Dad, I'm right and you're wrong," says the toddler. The Bible says that at some point in our Christian walk that we need to get off the teat and eat some real food. God's Word is that food. It is important to grow; it is important to know and reading His Holy Word is the only way that Christians eyes will be opened. What is the alternative? Staying weak in our faith, not growing, being ignorant? God has given us this amazing world and His amazing Word; He has given us His holy Spirit to carry with us daily in our soul. Pray earnestly that He will reveal His truths to you. Hint: He won't if you don't read His Word.

The amount of derision and ridicule about "God's Word" versus "the world's scientific proofs" proves that God is right; Satan and the world pushes back. That's how it works. The more proof that is given and explained, the louder the yelling gets, and then the anger rises to the level of being out of control. There is darkness in the world, darkness that we brought on ourselves, and some of that darkness is in the form of compromise. Many pastors already know that what I write is true and is confirmed in the Bible. There are also a lot of non-Christians who know the truth based on the obvious and simple experiments proving without doubt that we are not on a spinning globe. It's time to come out of the closet. God is calling us out through His written Word. Come out and own this! Or show that it is wrong, which is impossible. Truth is truth and lies are lies. The world lies, governments lie, people lie. God does not lie.

Like the phrase goes, "I am not of this world," and I want the next real and final world to get here sooner than later. I love my kids and grandkids and my wife, and I'd love to see my Dodgers win another World Series, but this world holds nothing for me. My entire family knows God and loves God—and we are all heading to heaven, so this life while an amazing experience and obviously important is not our final destination.

In October of 2015, I was invited by some old high school friends to join them on a hike of Yosemite's Half Dome. I had just turned fifty years old the previous May, and while I have always tried to keep myself in shape, I was not quite ready for an eighteen-hour hike that went almost straight up and straight back down. My buddies had been in training for months. I was a late invite as one of their sons had to back out at the last minute. I thought my best course of action was to do a lot of yoga. I had one week to get ready, and I did do yoga every day and all that stretching worked because I made it! Inserted is a picture from the top.

Eight thousand eight hundred thirty-nine feet above "sea level". For as far as you could see, we were the highest point. It was exhilarating, and it was a straight horizon, zero curve—flat, if you will. Once we got to the top, I separated myself from the group and pulled out a small Bible and read out loud the first chapter of Genesis. Tears flowed; the tears could not be helped.—God's wonder on display with no obstructions for three hundred sixty degrees. Breathtaking. No guess as to how far we could see, but it was a long way. I have been to the top of Half Dome and saw no curve. I have been in planes at 35,000 feet and never seen a curve. I have been to the oceans and only ever seen a straight-line horizon. I have seen curved rainbows but never seen water curve. I have seen beautiful sky blue through the moon just moments ago as we walked our dog on this lovely Saturday morning here in Southern California. I have seen the west sides of buildings when the sun was not yet visible in the east. I have used levels much more than the average person. I have been in planes flying and maintaining level over thousands of miles of our earth and oceans. I have done many experiments with water, and it's always the same—always level.

I have also prayed for guidance from the Creator of all (a lot). I have read many books detailing the math, experiments, and fallacies of a sphere planet like earth, and I have studied the Bible in depth, looking for the answers to my questions. In all of this, not one single proof of anything contradicting the Bible has been found. There are no experiments to prove that the world is round or that it is spinning. In fact, all proofs and experiments prove the opposite. The deception has been discovered, and there is indeed something called magic. What would you call a being that could make all of this with just a mere thought? Let there be light, and there was.

One law of God and science is that water will always seek its own level. Water is a magical substance, and without it, we die. Our human bodies are made up of two thirds water. Our brain is 75 percent $H2O$, our blood is 83 percent $H2O$, the heart is 79 percent $H2O$, bones are 22 percent $H2O$, muscles are 75 percent $H2O$, the liver is 86 percent $H2O$, and the kidneys are 83 percent $H2O$. Water can be frozen, liquid, and turned into steam. Oceans were made as our filtering system. It's used for powering mighty machinery and making delicious red juice that my grandkids love. Water is obviously very important to us humans.

I spent my living before retiring as a union plumber. I've joked in the past that I'm just a dumb plumber, but plumbers are not dumb. A union plumber has to go to five years of trade school and know a code book that is fairly thick with many rules and regulations. To work in hospitals takes more testing and certifications. I was in charge of the plumbing and mechanical systems for highrises, hospitals, jails, restaurants, hotels, Burger Kings, and Starbucks to name a few. I also got to help build rides and venues at Knott's Berry Farm, Universal Studios, and Disneyland. We installed pipes that carried water into and away from big tall buildings. I used a level most every day and am quite frankly disappointed in myself for not realizing how God's laws were working right in front of me and through my own hands for years.

Level is level.

There is a little bubble that shows me when I've installed something level and if it were not level then it would show me that too. In order to make water flow through a drainage pipe, we had to follow city codes that required the drainpipes to be on a grade of a quarter inch minimum per every foot of travel. If I installed a drainpipe at level, then water would just sit in the pipe never making its destination. Common sense and your eyes and a working level will tell you that water is level all around you.

Take a glass of water for example. No matter which way you tilt the glass, the water in the glass will be level. The water in a toilet is level, the water in a pool is level, the water in a lake is level, and the water in the ocean is level. We use the term *sea level* as a measuring tool, and if it were not level, then all of our calculations and elevations would not work. Mount Everest is 29,029 feet above sea level. If the earth were a curved ball, just where would we get a level reading from? God's laws at work. The oceans are the best example of level that there is on our world. I live in Southern California and grew up at the beach. I've witnessed many beautiful sunsets over the Pacific Ocean. As the sun moves away from me and out of my line of sight, it looks as if it's dropping into the horizon (it's not; more to come on that)—a very level horizon and a very horizontal horizon if you will. Water levels were the first levels man used when he started building buildings. Water levels are still used today in construction to hang doors. There is no better level than a water level because God's laws don't change.

Try your own experiment. Dump a five-gallon bucket of water (with or without salt) on any piece of ground you choose. The water will not stop moving until it has found a spot to sit and will always be level when it stops. Or take a clear tube and fill it with water and hold the tube up with both hands. If you raise your right hand higher than your left, the water in the tube will match the level of water in your left hand with pinpoint accuracy because water always seeks to be level. This is not in the Bible, but it is one of God's laws. And it's not just water, this law works with any liquid.

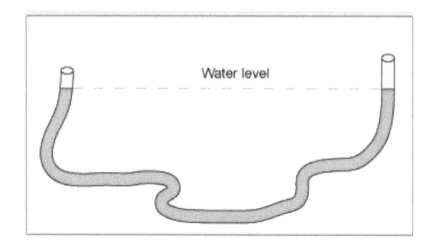

It has been observed that water does curve somewhat. A single drop of water can have a slight curve to it, like a rain drop, but add another drop or two and now it's just water that will go level, and a glass of water, toilet water, pool water, lake water, and ocean water are way more than a single drop. So if you have more than one drop of water, it will not curve. Our earth does not curve because water does not curve.

> *"For since the creation of the world His invisible attributes are clearly seen, being understood by the things that are made" (Romans 1:20).*

Mostly we have let the Bible verses speak for themselves because who am I thinking that I can word anything better than God's Word? But did you notice that in the verse above that it said, "His invisible attributes are clearly seen, being understood by the things that are made"?

God wants us to understand His work, and it is not hard to understand. God gave us senses, and we do our best to deny them. It is Satan who has corrupted the world and our understanding of it.

Unfortunately, we have no excuse for our ignorance.

Unless we are able to open our minds to the truth, the devil has won. Remember that term *cognitive dissonance* we needed to get back to? Well, it means that something is so ingrained in our brain that teaching our brain to consider something else is almost impossible. It would be easier to try and convince you that your name is not really your name than it would be to try and convince you that our world is not a spinning globe. The amount of indoctrination we received as children and the continued reinforcement as adults has made this possible and that is the power of cognitive dissonance.

Since our first days in the classroom, there were globes all around us. It is taught as fact, just like evolution (as Christians, do we believe in evolution? Surely not!) Satan is indeed cunning. Two plus two is four, and the world is round.

Sound familiar?

This phrase has been uttered by someone, somewhere, every single day for a very long time.

As Christians we believe in science. We should not believe in science fiction. All science and natural laws come from and are gifts from God. Two plus two is four. Water seeks its own level. The sun rises, and the sun sets. These are terms we use today. My weather app tells me when sunset is and when sunrise is. Science always proves the existence of God. Our human bodies prove the existence of God and science. Every person ever born has their own unique DNA, which is now used to catch criminals. It's foolproof; no one else has your DNA. Have you ever noticed that not one person looks like another person anywhere? Even identical twins are not identical. That is some artist that can come up with billions of different faces. If we were able to have all the very best artists throughout all history together at one time and gave them a thousand years each to draw faces, they would run out of ideas. God is never out of ideas when it comes to individuals. He knitted us together in our own uniqueness in our mother's womb. God is unlike any other artist; He has an infinite imagination and never runs out unique designs for our bodies and our faces.

More science. The straight lines on a flat plane are buildings and the same for the straight lines on the ball. The distance between the buildings on a flat plane will be the same at the top of the building as the bottom of the building. Not so with buildings on a curved ball. There is all the proof you need; we do not live on a curve. Someone please explain how a level works on a round earth. Hey, NASA, how about a picture of our earth showing buildings upside down? That would be cool—an untrue lie, but cool. Level is level and plumb is plumb.

Science does not lie, Satan does. Bill Nye "the science guy" taught us on Saturday mornings that we live on a "curved planet" and that when a boat disappears over the horizon of the ocean, it is because it went behind the curve of the world (these old TV clips can easily be viewed on YouTube). A round, spinning globe is at the core of the world's belief system and for controlling the minds of the masses and enslaving them to the delight of Satan, and he has many minions who pretend to know things that we ignorant folk don't— Nye, Tyson, Freud, Darwin, Einstein, etc.

Well, the science guy was wrong, and he has led a generation of kids over a dark curve indeed. Today we have technology that I'm sure the world wishes we didn't have; in our hands, we can pull up an app for a level, and it works. How does a cellphone app level work? It works the same way airplane instrumentation works; it needs a level surface to read off of. The problem is people have their faces stuck in that technology for all the wrong reasons. We have cameras that can shoot pictures further than ever before. The boat is still there. With the new cameras we have, filming and zooming in on objects over sixty miles away, we can zoom out and not see the boat anymore and then zoom in, and there it is again. It didn't disappear over the curve!

Hey, science guy, it just got too far for our eyes to see. Finally, technology that does some good. If we were taught these truths as young impressionable children, then the cognitive dissonance would be strong in the opposite direction. Simple, logical, and easy experiments that a child can see and understand were not shown to us on purpose. Instead we were told about gravity, but no one showed us how this "gravity" works. We were taught that the world is round but with no proof, no experiments.

What else were we lied to about? Science tells us that our "planet" is thirty thousand miles in circumference. Let's just say they are right for the purpose of exposing it to be a lie. Based on that information, if we travel one mile we will lose eight inches of vision in that mile due to "the curve," and on mile two, the math tells us that we have to square it, so we now have lost sixty-four inches of vision due to the "curve." That said, traveling ninety miles, we would lose approximately five thousand four hundred two feet of vision.

Note this: in the picture below that the island of Oahu is ninety miles from the Kauai Airport. Five thousand four hundred two feet of lost vision due to the "mythical curve" would make this impossible to see. And the picture was taken over some very flat, level water.

There is no curve to our earth, and it does not move. God and science don't lie. When we can no longer see something on a flat plane, it is because it is out of our line of sight. The sun is in our firmament and moves across our sky until it is no longer visible, then the night takes over. When the sun is at high noon, it looks like it is as high as it is going to get, then it looks like it drops. It does not drop; it moves away from us, so it looks like it is getting lower. It's perspective. A telephone pole right next to you looks tall because it is, but look down the line and see how small all the other poles seem to be. You can hold your thumb and index finger up and look at those tall poles in between them. You can be less than five feet from a friend and look through the same fingers and fit their face into it.

Perspective!

The sun looks like it is at its highest point at high noon. As it travels away from you, it looks lower and lower just like the telephone poles. The truth is right in front of our faces and our senses, but we either deny them or don't think about them much. Our sun moves at four degrees an hour, always has and always will. It's how the sundials worked. Our earth is huge, and the sun is on its circuit above us in the firmament that God created for us. It is in the Bible. It is proven by science. It is proven by the natural laws of God.

Even with the Bible and science and proof, most people cannot get over what they think they "know" to be true. His Word says that if we pray for wisdom, He will give it (*James 1:5*). Know that it wasn't easy for me to overcome my own cognitive dissonance, but I consider myself to be an openminded, free thinker who wants only to know the truth. Sheep are led astray because they are dumb. Choose not to be dumb. The only proof on the other side is Hollywood films and doctored pictures provided by the government and NASA, which the government runs, and the public-school system (also ran by the government) that indoctrinates our young minds for thirteen years before we go off to a most likely liberal college. They wouldn't lie, would they?

That is a lot to overcome. That's how good a job Satan did with all those movies, books, and TV shows. Just like in 1938 with the *War of the Worlds* broadcast, people are now primed to believe in anything with the exception of the truth. I am also very aware that if I could deduce what the Bible is saying about what we live in, then people a lot smarter than I also know these truths. I am more than a little disappointed that the Christian church has not stood up on this issue by now. Millions of pastors and hundreds of thousands of churches in American history, and no one got this? Hard to believe.

My goodness, it's 2020, and we are debating against the Word of God about rudimentary topics such as whether the sun moves or the earth moves. No matter, the issue must be forced. The first thing my son said to me after proofreading and helping edit this book for me was, and I quote, "You're going to get yourself shot." I have had the same thought. Scary times we live in—that there is a topic that can and will induce hatred and violence is shocking. Mere words will lead us to these dark times ahead, the Bible is proof of that. But we are saved by grace through faith, and when Jesus decides that my time is up here on this earth, then so be it. Until then, I am invincible and so are you.

> *"Do not fear those who can kill the body but are not able to kill the soul, fear only God who can destroy both body and soul in hell" (Matthew 10:28).*

My hope is that more people will accept this truth and know that you are indeed invincible until God is done with you here on earth, and we are not in charge of when our time is up either. Knowing this and embracing it will free you up to life your life in ways you've never known before. Only when you are prepared to die are you truly prepared to live.

# CHAPTER 5

## Airplanes

*Thick clouds are a covering to him, that he sees not;*
*and he walketh in the circle of heaven.*

*—Job 22:14*

Let's talk about airplanes. Yes, this book is directed toward born-again Christians, but what I know about this topic is that if you're going to engage with people about it, you better be prepared with as many answers as possible to every conceivable type of question. People do not give up their cognitive dissonance without a fight.

Proof can be sitting in front of their face, and they will want more. That is why time and space is being spent on topics outside the Bible like the ones we've talked about so far—level water, curve of earth, programming our minds, and now planes. Besides, born-again Christians fly on planes too.

Fact: there are zero plane flights around the "backside of the earth" because there is no backside, and flight patterns are easy to look up. If you want to get from Australia to Alaska, you'll have many layovers because flights basically only go east to west. Flight patterns can be found online with an easy search. Here is what you will find.

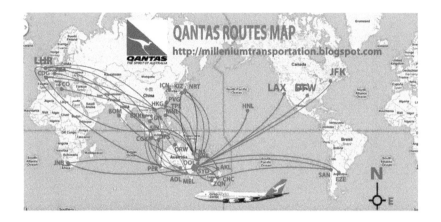

Also, if our airplanes were traveling over a curved planet, pilots would have to tip the nose of their planes down every few seconds to maintain altitude. Remember the math we did between the Hawaiian Islands? It works in the air too.

Every plane has an altimeter on the control panel that the pilot keeps "level" once flying altitude has been met. Wikipedia defines an altimeter as a crucial instrument on an airplane that keeps an object above a fixed level surface! More proof that most people will shrug off and look for the next question.

*"But what about this or that?"* Never satisfied, always trying to find another question. Cognitive dissonance is powerful.

Take a plastic level with you on your next flight in your carry-on bag and put it on the floor during your flight once altitude is met. It will stay level even on the longest of flights. Planes fly over planes (earth below). Our own verbiage outs the truth. Once again, the case could be rested on this one scientific fact that uses a scientific tool (the altimeter). Did you know that this extremely important tool is used on every single airplane everywhere and that in order for it to work, the plane must maintain level balance over the level surface of oceans and the earth?

But secrets have to be kept; the lies can't get out.

"Hello, America (world), this is your evening news, this just out. Everything you've ever been taught is a lie!"

Not ever going to ever happen. Christians need to be "woke" as the new slang says. Christians need to challenge the truths that have been unearthed from His Holy Word. Christians need force the issue. It's a darn important one. Show where God's Word is wrong! It's not. Are we as Christians too afraid to own it? If the Bible gets it so very wrong about a moving sun, then can we trust anything in it? Do we believe in the talking donkey? It's in the Bible. Where is our faith? What do we believe?

My wife and I and some friends were fortunate enough to take a vacation this past year that required a long flight over the Pacific Ocean. I was lucky enough to get a window seat which I always like. Our flight left at midnight out of LAX (you get better deals leaving on the red eye). I fell asleep and woke up just as the sun was coming up. How beautiful it was,—nothing but ocean and the sun. We were up around thirty-five thousand feet, which is normal flying altitude, and there were no clouds. I was able to see the horizon perfectly and at eye level—a very straight, no-curve horizon and a beautiful moving sun coming up over it.

Remember how we talked about perspective? Out that small window, I was able to see hundreds and hundreds of miles of that horizontal, level horizon. Zero curve. On your next flight, don't forget your level and try to get a window seat. The sun moves, the earth won't move, buildings are level all over the earth, water seeks to be level, planes fly over a level surface, and again, there is no curve to our world. This is logic and this is science. We maintained thirty-five thousand feet for the entire trip because the pilot kept his altimeter level with the level ocean and level earth below us—never tipping the nose of the plane down to stay with the curve. If the earth were a ball, then the plane staying level would not stay level with the earth below and fly off into "outer space."

Shocking truth: science does not lie and always proves the existence of God. The world and Satan always try to turn it around. As the old TV show used to say, "The truth is out there."

The horizon will always rise to your eye level no matter how tall or short you are. Even if you're up on a ladder looking out the window of a sixty-story building, or standing on a beach, or thirty-five thousand feet in the air flying, just look out the window. The horizon is always at your eye level. Same for the six-foot-six man next to you or the four-foot-nine little old lady in front of you.

Try this experiment for yourself. Take the tallest or shortest person you know with you to your local beach. Take as tall a ladder with you as you can and put the taller person at the top of the ladder and the shorter person can sit or squat down. Now both of you look out at the horizon and tell each other where the horizon level is. The horizon will be right at each persons eye level, every time, no matter how high you climb.

In my last year as a union plumber, we had a job working in a building in Century City, California. We were on the forty-first floor and had an amazing ocean view. My rather tall fellow worker was up on a ten-foot ladder, and I was standing on the floor. I asked him to look out the window and also asked him where the horizon was in his vision. He said it was level with his eyes. It was level with mine too. We switched places, and he was shocked to find it was still the same. He even laid on the floor to see if it would change. It did not.

Not being satisfied with just that, we retrieved a four-foot level from the toolbox and pushed it up against the glass and lined it up with the horizon line of the ocean. Perfectly level. We had to be more than ten miles from the beach, and the horizon was many miles further than that. The amount of ocean that was able to be seen in the distance from left to right had to be at least twenty-plus miles or more, and there was no curve. Zero curve. The level was as true as the ocean was level. A $50 four-foot level made a believer that day—not a born-again believer but a believer in that we have been lied to by the world.

But why? Now that is a big question, and we will answer it.


A very smart man once had this observation.

"I fear the day when the technology overlaps with our humanity. The world will only have a generation of idiots"

We've had the greatest generation—the baby boomers, Generation X, and Millennials. Welcome, Generation Idiots. We are here, and that observation from a very smart man is proven correct. Our faces are stuck swiping right and left never looking up.

That same vacation, we had a great time, and we were with two of our best friends that we have known for over thirty years. So they are real good friends that know us pretty darn well. On a tropical vacation with lots of time together both on the beach and in the plane, lots of topics come up. Yes, you guessed it—this topic.

This example is identical to the reaction that always happens when this subject is talked about. This is not polite company, these are lifelong friends that know us as well as anyone could. Cognitive dissonance always has the same reactions, however, with friends or with strangers. First, you get laughed at. Second is anger. If you get to third you may get someone who actually thinks about it and opens their minds to the possibility that it could be true and just maybe they have been wrong about something this big for their entire life.

At the risk of ruining our awesome vacation, I brought it up. We talked for a while about it. First came the laughs and mild ridicule, then my friend's wife got mad and was having no more of it. The husband got to the third stage. Pretty good if you ask me, one for two. At least he was willing to think about it. That vacation was over a year ago now and I'm pleased to say that those friends have cast off the devil and his lies about our world and have embraced Gods Holy Word that declares the moving sun and that our earth is set on firm foundations and will not move.

This same situation came up with a room full of my family members not too long ago. FYI, we are a close-knit Christian family that should be able to handle any subject matter. Nope. Let's just say that I was asked to not broach this topic again in a family setting. Hence, the writing of this book.

Think about that. I've got three grown kids in their thirties and seven grandkids. I was told not to try and teach my own grandkids about my beliefs—beliefs that come straight out of the Bible! That's the job Satan has done with this bullcrap indoctrination. My oldest grandchild is six, and *knows* that the earth is a round, spinning ball. Now how would a six-year-old just know that? And did Papa just say "bullcrap"? another FYI, I am not a "holier-than-thou" Christian, I am a real guy who is passionate about the Word of God, and in that passion I can, on occasion, use a colorful word or two. Most all of those words have been omitted (you should've read the first draft) so not to offend, but sometimes when you just want to drive a passionate point home, a well-placed curse word does the trick. This paragraph is one of those occasions. Passion is understandable, the emotional level of humans can get volatile when the task is to break through *cognitive dissonance* of this kind. It triggers a deep anger that exists because deep down we know that we have been lied to. At the same time we feel like we are being personally attacked but we don't know why we feel the way we do, the trick is to somehow put emotions aside as just look at the facts.

How did I know that the world was round when I was young? How did you? And why? Were we given any chance to believe otherwise? Maybe one of my well-intentioned teachers could have taken us on a field trip to the beach and set up two ladders with a long, firm, straight plank in between them and placed a long level on that plank and lined the horizon of the Pacific Ocean up with it and let us all see that it is perfectly level over miles and miles. Zero curve. Now why would they do that? They just might get questioned on evolution next. Can't let that happen, can they?

So let's go back to sixth grade. I've done that same experiment here for you. There is no trick photography

Simple experiments that can be done and proven beyond any shadow of doubt by a sixth grader. This experiment and many others can easily be taught and shown to children just as easily as they can be indoctrinated into a lie. And you and I never even got one simple experiment to prove that the earth is round, did we? For more experiments, tests, and proofs, I direct you to the books by Edward Hendrie *The Greatest Lie on Earth* and *One Hundred Proofs That the Earth Is Not a Globe* by WM Carpenter, as well as *Earth Is Not a Globe* by Samuel Rowbotham. While I believe Edward Hendrie to be a Christian, I am not sure of the other two. They are long dead, and their experiments and math equations are done from a purely scientific view. In this book, the point is to come at the born-again believer and the leaders of our churches from a mostly biblical view in order to put this biblical truth out into the world, but some basic scientific principals were needed to add a measure of worldly gravitas to the truth that was given to us through His Word. Rowbotham said this, "If one is guided by evidence and reason, and influenced by love of the truth and consistency, then one can no longer maintain that the earth is a globe."

Trust your senses. When something smells bad, don't eat it. When something looks bad, don't wear it. When a friend says you need to brush your teeth, go floss, brush, brush again, and use mouthwash. Schedule a teeth cleaning with your dentist too. Your own senses will very rarely lie to you. We feel like we are not moving because we are not moving. The sun looks like it's moving because it's moving. We can see blue through the moon because it's translucent. The horizon looks level because its level. Rainbows are arch-shaped because they reflect off something that's arch-shaped and huge. We can see the west side of a building even though the sun is not yet up in the east because the hard-looking glass sky is reflecting the sun's light on it. God said that the sun moves so the sun moves.

*Gospel Earth* is a book of Gods truths based on the Holy Word of God. Readers are encouraged to place these truths right next to the actual Word of God and examine them. I am a faithful Christian who up to the point of writing this book has been a respected member of my church and community. I have not taken any of God's Word out of context. I have not twisted His Holy Word to match what the world wants us to believe, it's the other way around. Right is wrong, white is black, and two plus two probably doesn't even equal four anymore.

Science was created by God; it's always been here working and doing its thing before we even knew what a fraction was. He alone created all that we have, He alone created all the mathematics of our world. We have no cars, cellphones, planes, trains, computers, microwaves, or even food had God not placed all that we needed in the ground for us to find and utilize. Two plus two equals four because God set it up that way—not you, not me, and not some scientist. There was no big bang, there is no evolution, and there is no evidence to support those theories. There is also no evidence indicating that we live on a spinning, round globe.

We saw in Genesis that man was created very smart. The writing of the first book of the Bible, arguably the first book ever written, was masterful, descriptive, and eloquent. To deny God's work is to deny God and to accept Satan's twisted version of it is sin. Who are we to interpret what God "really" meant to say when He said that the sun moves? Where were we when He laid the foundations of the world? Where were you when He stretched out the sky like a hard-molten looking glass? Where were we when He set limits for how far humans are allowed to go? Where were you when this beautiful world was created for us? Were you there? Where you an eyewitness? Did you cause the dawn to know its place that it might take hold of the ends of the earth? Did you take darkness to its territory that you may know the path to its home? Have you seen the gates of death? Has it been revealed to you? He hardened the waters like stone and froze the deep. Did you? All these questions are taken from Job 38. We were not there, and Moses was not there either, but we trust what he wrote in Genesis because it came from God Himself and through Moses—just like the entire written Bible did through various authors, word for word. Do we believe the Bible? Do our pastors and leaders believe the Bible or just portions of it? If the Bible is wrong about the sun moving, could it be wrong about other things? Do people rise from the dead?

That's a good one. It's a slippery slope indeed. *Job 38:2* says, "*Who is this who darkens counsel by words without knowledge?*" Basically, who are you? You question Me? Seriously? You talk and know nothing of My greatness. You don't know My ways. You have no knowledge. Sit down, listen up, prepare yourself like a man, and I'll tell you how I did things. God said this to Job! Are we so full of ourselves that we consider ourselves to be better than Job? We must listen to Gods Holy Word for we are no one.

We cannot just take verses or passages out of the Bible to use as we see fit. It is not ours to do that with. If God Himself spoke all these words and put them in the order that He wanted, just like He did our world, who are we to deny it and claim another truth? If you still hold fast to the firm belief that the sun does not move and that a round globe spins, then you call God a liar. Do not call God a liar. Our world is held up by Him. "*He hangs the earth on nothing*" (*Job 26:7*). The spell must be broken that our world is under concerning our earth. There is nothing on, in, or above the earth that God is not responsible for. He has told us in His Word exactly what He made for us to enjoy and live in. He made the world as to protect us as well. It may look like fantasy, but below is a biblical rendition of what our world looks like according to the Bible side by side with the globe that we've all grown up with. Which one looks more like fantasy? Consider what we would think if we had been taught all of our life that the biblical view is correct, that instead of having little globes spinning on our desk as children, we had little snow globes that showed a sun and a moon and stars in it sitting there instead. Oh, well the world couldn't put up with that. Why, that's indoctrination!

That is exactly what the world has done with the globes everywhere you look,—indoctrination of the most sinister kind. And you and I, we're its target, and you and I remain the target.

Here's a fun fact for you airplane buffs. The SR-71 Blackbird has a top speed of 2,436 mph (Mach 3.2) and can climb to a max altitude of 85,000 ft. And all calculations assume a flat and nonrotating earth. The DPS equations of motion use four assumptions that simplify the program while maintaining its fidelity for most maneuvers and applications: point-mass modeling, nonturbulent atmosphere, zero side forces, and a nonrotating earth (taken from the government website: www.nasa.gov/centers/dryden/pdf/88507main H-2179.pdf).

Think about it, something moving this fast could not calculate for a round spinning world. The smallest of errors would have this plane flying off into "outer space," or crashing into the earth, before a pilot knew that he had made a mistake!

# CHAPTER 6

---

# Rainbows and Unicorns

*But my horn shalt thou exalt like the horn of the
Unicorn: I shall be anointed with fresh oil.*

*—Psalm 92:10*

Rainbows and unicorns? Okay, well, everyone knows that unicorns are not real. Right? By the time my granddaughters are old enough to read this, they will know there aren't any unicorns around, and thankfully, I won't be the one to shatter their dreams. But they were real at some point. Look up *Numbers 23:22* and *24:8*, along with *Job 39:9–10* and *Psalm 29:6* and *92:10*.

Rainbows are certainly still around, and similar to the elusive unicorn, you'll never be able to catch one or find the pot of gold at the end of one. God flooded the world by opening the doors of heaven (the waters above us) (*Genesis 1:6; Psalm 148:4*).

In the time of Noah, God caused a rainbow to appear as a sign after the flood of the earth that He would never open those doors again to flood the earth. It takes three elements to create a rainbow. We've all seen this magical sight and taken it for granted. It should not be taken for anything but an awesome display of Gods wonder. Rainbows are not rare but they are also not common, and they are always beautiful. Those three elements to create a rainbow are light, water, and a reflective surface. *Job 37:18* says, *"Can you help God spread out the skies as hard as a cast metal mirror?"*

There is your reflective surface, and it's a big one. Fact: a rainbow cannot be created indoors without the use of a mirror, and it will reflect only the shape of that mirror. A rainbow outside is never in the shape of a square or a triangle or a straight line. Outdoors with no mirrors around and no shiny buildings around to reflect off of, we get a beautiful arch-shaped rainbow. The hard reflective and protective firmament above us is dome-shaped and reflects the water in the air along with God's sun and creates a rainbow. Man did not create this, God did.

Seriously? Now I'm suggesting that we live in a snow globe. Well, there's your globe, I suppose. *Genesis 9:13* says, *"I set my rainbow in the clouds and it shall be a sign of the covenant between Me and the earth."* By the way, the word *earth* is used so many times in the Bible, it's mind-blowing, but never once is the word *planet* used. I think if our Creator, whom we believe in as Bible-believing Christians, created an astronomical ever-expanding planetary universe, we would know about it from His Word.

The fact that all these truths and scientific facts have to be explained like this is a scary example that this world is being controlled by the lord of darkness. We should have known about this as kids, performed experiments, and gone on field trips. Instead, we were fed lies and indoctrinated into a nonbiblical cult of science fiction. We are blind to the truth. Subtle lies mixed with truth is the reason there are millions and millions of humans trapped in the aforementioned cults.

Attention all, born-again believers. Just try going up to a JW or an LDS member or a Muslim and tell them that they are wrong, that most of what they believe in is a lie from Satan himself, and see what happens. By the way, we are called to do just that. We know that no one comes to the Father except through Jesus the Son. Furthermore, we are required to share this with the lost (*Mark 16:15*).

The Bible says that there is only one way to the Father (*John 14:6*). Jesus said, *"I am the way, the truth, and the life; no man comes to the Father, but by me."*

Period.

End of conversation.

God Himself, the Creator of all things, said that His sun moves. There can be only one God. There can be only one truth.

> *"Narrow is the path and there are few who find it"*
> *(Matthew 7:14).*

This passage speaks of salvation and the truth it represents. It also speaks of just plain truth. God gave us truth and natural laws. Let's look at some more indoctrination.

Which animal is faster. A roadrunner or a coyote?

If your answer was a roadrunner, why did you think that?

Answer: Saturday morning cartoons.

Fact: roadrunners' top speed is twenty miles per hour, and a coyote can reach up to forty-three miles per hour. I think old Wiley Coyote got a bum rap. Beep-beep! That was a silly cartoon meant to entertain kids, but I saw a lot of those episodes as a child, and I didn't realize until I was older that it was wrong and manipulating to some degree.

The world has been indoctrinating the masses like this for a very long time. Below are some pictures taken from frames of cartoons and movies. Disturbing at the very least.

(The Disney and other sexual cartoon pictures have been removed for explicit content.)

We were lied to, and we are lied to all the time about non-important stuff and very important stuff. Remember, Satan mixes the truth with lies. You can see that even in children's cartoons, agendas are pushed, and disturbing sexual images are left in front of our children's eyes. It is up to us as followers of Christ to reject these messages, propaganda, and the lies forced upon us. We've been manipulated about much more than the shape of our world, but it all comes from the same source. Satan himself.

The lies and half-truths that have been engrained in our little skulls of mush as children are so very hard to overcome and will be even harder for our kids if we don't wake them up to the truth now.

We have been programmed, and we have to fight back. I look up into the beautiful sky and see a brilliant blue. I wonder, as maybe you have, why is it blue? It's a simple question that kids have asked their parents for ages.

We were taught that the oceans reflect up to the sky, and that's why it's blue. But wait, water is clear and air is clear and if the ocean is reflecting blue, then why aren't the white clouds blue? And why then, when a stormy day is blustering and the clouds break just a little, we can still see a brilliant blue above all the dark storm clouds?

God gave us all the different colors of trees, birds, fish, foods, dyes for fabrics, animals, our hair, our eyes, and more. The sky, a strong hard protective mirror as indicated in *Job 37:18*, is the color blue.

Here's another simple scientific experiment you can try. Go to an ocean or lake and take as big a container as you want and scoop up the water. Do the same with some clean fresh air. Take these containers home and study them to see if there are any signs of the color blue or any color at all for that matter. Of course, all you will see is clear transparent properties. Clear is not a color, is it? Yet in the same clear blue sky, we can see a rainbow with all seven primary colors, don't we? And always in the same order! Oh, thank you Lord for your promises and awesome displays of grandeur.

We truly live in a magical place. Alas, there are no unicorns left, but there is grand simplicity to our world. The oxymoron of the ages—complex simplicity! The sky looks blue because it is. A rainbow is created because it is light being reflected through water off the ceiling of the blue arch shaped sky. Water seeks its own level because our Lord created scientific properties to it that do not allow it to curve or bend. Coyotes run faster than roadrunners. Our protection from the waters above was "cast *like a hard-molten looking glass*," as the Bible states.

# CHAPTER 7

## United Nations, Antarctica, and Cellphone Culture

*Woe unto them that call evil good and good evil;
that put darkness for light and light for darkness;
that put bitter for sweet, and sweet for bitter.*

*—Isaiah 5:20*

Speaking of God's awesome display of grandeur, let us consider Antarctica for a moment. It is the only land mass that is not owned by anyone nor has any native human population. Now, I have never been to Antarctica nor will I be going anytime soon, but we can learn a lot through the miracle of the world wide web, web cams, and other people's observations and findings.

There are a lot of questions about Antarctica:

Can anyone go as far as they want to once they reach Antarctica?

What is the Antarctica treaty and who's involved in it?

Why does the United Nations flag and the World Health Organization logo use a flat earth model map?

Where is Antarctica on this map?

Are the world governments that signed onto the Antarctica treaty trying to hide something from us?

Who is Admiral Richard Byrd and what did he discover there?

Who is Captain James Cook and what did he discover about Antarctica?

Here are some quick answers to the above questions.

1. I don't know if anyone can go as far as they want to once they reach Antarctica. One it would take a lot of time and money and bravery to try. It is common knowledge that there are military bases there belonging to more countries than just the USA, and the speculation and rumors are that anyone trying to go too far will be turned around at gunpoint.

2. The Antarctica treaty is still in place today after more than seventy years and many countries are involved. Most treaties don't last ten minutes.

3. The United Nation in fact does use a flat earth map as their symbol and in that symbol are thirty-three sections, a number worshiped by Masonic members. Also, the World Health Organization uses a similar symbol adding a serpent wrapped around a pole and the same thirty-three sections.

4. Admiral Byrd was the real Indiana Jones and the youngest Navy man to become an Admiral. He led two major expeditions to Antarctica bringing back incredible information. Operation "high jump" and operation "fishbowl". High jump referring to the massive ice walls that had to be conquered and fishbowl referring to a hard-looking glass sky. It is another easy search to pull up his name on YouTube and watch his live television Q and A from the 1940's where he says a little too much and is soon dead thereafter.

5. Captain James Cook was a British explorer who sailed next to the ice walls of Antarctica in the 1700's. He and his crew sailed over 60,000 nautical miles as they circumnavigated the ice walls never finding an inlet or an outlet.

I hope you will research some of these names and go down a few of the rabbit holes that I have in my research for this book. However, I am solely writing this book based on what I know God's Word says, and it says that He has set limits to how far we can go. Frozen ice and thousands of miles of sub-below temperatures and storms would be a great deterrent for keeping mankind away from what God apparently does not want us finding.

Has anyone ever flown over Antarctica and across the supposed three thousand miles of ice? Or did they just fly in circles?

The Word of God says that the foundations of the world were seen at one point in history and that we are being protected by a hard metal glass called the sky. *Amos 9:6* says, "*He who builds His layers in the sky, and has founded His strata in the earth.*" An entire book can be written on Antarctica and its secrets, but I am not qualified at this time to be that author who writes it, so do some of your own homework if you're interested, you'll find heated debate all over the internet on this topic. It is truly an interesting topic, which I needed to at least mention in this book.

Bottom line is this: if we are so stubborn and prideful that we will not even consider the biblical proof and scientific proof laid out so far, then all of Satan's tricks have worked. Do you believe in God's Word? Did He say exactly what He wanted said in His Word? Do you think that Satan is trying his best to undermine God's Word?

> "*The earth is the Lords, and all its fullness, the world and those who dwell in it. For He has founded it upon the seas and established it upon the waters*" (*Psalm 24:1–2*).

The ice walls of Antarctica are real and can be easily looked up and viewed on YouTube. They are real, and they are doing their job keeping the seas and waves inside our protective system. The proud waves stop here. With today's technology we can easily pull up these videos on our phones while driving or pretending to pay attention to someone at dinner.

People don't care that they have been lied to, we are too busy with the practice of self. The cellphone is in everyone's face all day, every day. We are being programmed yet again with this tool, and we are programming our kids. Heck, my oldest grandkid is only six, and she can fly through her mom's cellphone and pull up anything she wants to watch faster than most adults!

A few years back, I was at my sister-in-law's home and my niece who was around twenty at the time was on her cellphone while we were having dinner. Not talking, just on it. She set it down for a moment, and I reached over and picked it up. She freaked out. I continued to hold it for a while teasing her then it made a buzz sound indicating that she had just received a text. Now she really started to flip out. She had to know immediately what was happening. I teased her for a little while longer but finally gave it back. She flicked her fingers with amazing speed to find out what was in the text. It said, "What's up?"

Important stuff.

We take selfies, lie on Facebook about how great everything is, we post on Instagram to impress others, and people even send sexual images of themselves out into the world. You can Google or YouTube anything. You don't need to really know anything, it's just all there in a handheld device that can cost up to a $1000, and we are never satisfied and rarely use these things for anything important.

Remember the flip phone or the Razor phone? So cool!

That was until the new phone came out, and now that flip phone is garbage. We watch movies on them, we bank and buy on them, we do everything on them and freak out when we misplace them. I've seen whole families sitting in a restaurant, and every one of them (moms and dads too) sitting there, not talking to each other but with their face stuck in this little black box, dutifully spending hours and hours swiping their life away and being controlled by the information fed to them on this device. Once again, on an iPhone, your default screensaver is a round, spinning globe being pushed into your face. I have a cellphone too but with very few apps. I have a Bible app, a weather app, and a news app. There is also a feature that lets me know exactly how much time I spend on the phone. Yes, the same news app that puts pictures and fake news of all things space in front of me.

We would do well to spend at least as much time in our Bible as we do on the cell phone. Some programming can be good. Having a mind full of wisdom sent from above doesn't even compare to the latest cat video.

> *"For wisdom is better than rubies, and all things one may desire cannot be compared with her" (Proverbs 8:11).*

A major problem with the world we live in today is the amount of power we have given to our governments, our media, and the ways in which we consume their information. The mainstream media would never lie to us, would they? Our governments wouldn't lie on a massive scale, would they? Everything on the internet is truth, isn't it? Far from it. God's Word is absolute truth, and it has been proven time and time again throughout the ages.

# CHAPTER 8

## Flat Earth and False Gods

*For the invisible things of him from the creation of
the world are clearly seen, being understood by the
things that are made, even his eternal power and
Godhead; so that they are without excuse.*

*—Romans 1:20*

Okay. So, let's just say it because it's what has been inferred to
since the start of this book.

Flat earth.

We are so programmed that just saying the words *flat earth*
sparks derision and ridicule. The masses have been programmed so
that a visceral response is the only response you'll ever get at the
raising of this topic. It cannot be talked about in polite company. As
already mentioned, it has caused friction in my own family (a Bible-
believing Christian family, mind you) and is a primary reason I began
writing this book.

If you can't talk about it, then write about it. I have tried, in
vain, to talk with pastors about this. I am in turn labeled a kook for
reading the Bible and believing the Bible, imagine that. I can't even
get a legitimate discussion going with a pastor about it. Christians
today are afraid to be labeled as a "flat-earther." The devil and his
minions have propagandized people to associate the term with being

ignorant: says Edward Hendrie on page 331 of his book, *The Greatest Lie on Earth*. Edward Hendrie's books were an incredible help with my research. His books lay out all the math and proofs of a stationary earth in enormous detail. This book you're reading now is a mere rallying cry to the Christian church today. However, absolutely every scientific experiment agrees with the words found in the Christian Bible.

With all the Bible verses already laid out and the 100 percent factual easy-to-perform experiments with water and levels and airplane instrumentation and observation, you would think that at least some openminded persons would at least question the "norm." If you are one of those, then I applaud you for considering it, but my experience is this: when a point is made that is irrefutable, the person or persons I am talking to will quickly try to move the conversation to another question or point.

Wait a minute, what about this fact!

What about water and levels and math and observation and the Bible for crying out loud!

What more proof will you need?

What answer will satisfy?

Is there anything that can bust through your cognitive dissonance?

What will be the breaking point for you as a born-again Christian? Which Bible verse? Which answered prayer? They reply, "Well, that's just the way people perceived things way back then. The sun looked like it was moving so that's what they wrote."

My goodness, that's a very big error in our Bible, don't you think? We as humans don't want to be thought of as being outside the normal. Fact: you're already outside the normal if you believe in God and the Bible. People get made fun of that are outside the normal. What is normal? For most of the history of this world, it was taught and thought that our world was flat and that the sun was moving. What happened and when did it happen that it was changed to a round, spinning ball? There were no spaceships or technology to prove it, just astronomers and philosophers! Take a close look at our "planets" in our "solar system"—more round balls. Also, let's take notice of the names of these other planetary systems and "worlds."

1. Neptune, named after the Roman god of the sea. Identified with the Greek deity Poseidon, son of the Titan Cronus (the Roman god Saturn) and brother of Zeus (the Roman god Jupiter). Can I please remind you "Thou shall have no other gods before Me"? Commandment number one. Here is a picture of Neptune. Not looking very real, is it? They say this "planet" is billions of miles away, but we have amazing fake video and pictures of it.

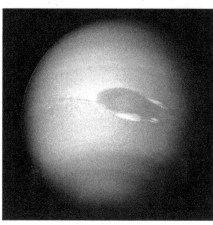

2. Uranus, named for the personification of heaven and the son and husband of Gaea in Greek mythology. Son and husband, huh? The devil at work again. Here are some pictures of this "planet"

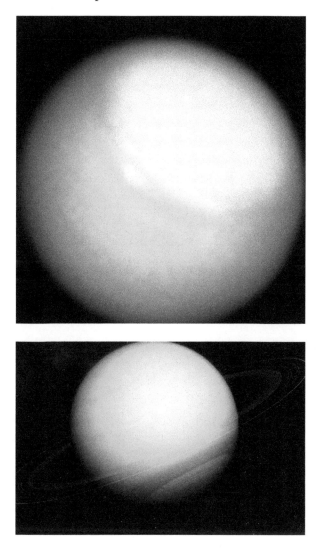

they don't even look like the same "planet" real or fake? Where is the ring in the first picture?

3. Saturn, named for the Roman god of agriculture and father of Zeus. Eight hundred eighty-seven million miles away from earth. Again, here are some fake pictures for you to enjoy.

4.  Jupiter, named after a Roman god, god of the sky. Have you noticed yet the common theme in the names of these fake planets? Everyone wants to be a god and deny the one true God. Here's your pictures.

5.  Mars, a Roman god. Imagine that, another god. A god of war, in fact. All of this is steeped in Satanic worship of the devil himself.

6. Venus, a Roman goddess. Hey, we got a female god now, cool. She is identified with the Greek goddess of love Aphrodite and is very naked in all the images shown.

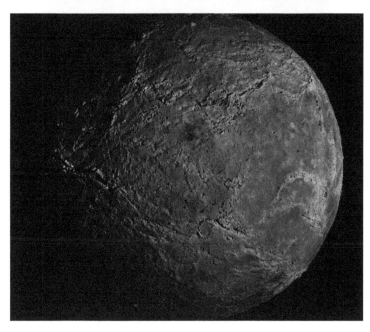

7. Mercury, a Roman god. Also quite naked. I am glad that this ends our little trip through the so-called planets. Here is your final fake, not real, propaganda pictures of a "world" that does not exist.

These are pictures from NASA. They look different than the pictures of the "planets" from earlier in the book, don't they? Something else to consider: what are the names of the "space flights" we supposedly went on?

Mercury program. Gemini program. Apollo program. Artemis program.

The theme is continuous. Why is earth not named after a Roman god? I know it's English, but I think that it is cool that the word *earth* rearranged spells *heart*. God's heart must break over man's feeble attempt to rewrite God's history and change what He did and make up planets that don't exist and call them names of other gods.

Earth—"the only frontier." Here is another picture from NASA of earth that looks completely different than the ones previously shown. What gives? Does the earth keep changing the way it looks? Do continents shift and change size and shapes? Forget "global warming," we need to worry about "global changing"!

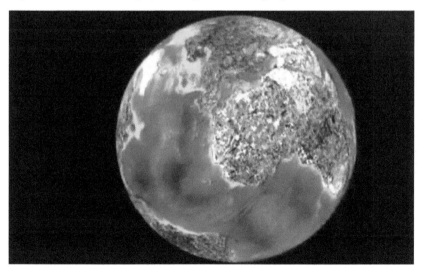

The creation of this book utilized many resources including many versions of the Bible and a Bible app called the Blue Letter Bible, Strong's Concordance, several Bible dictionaries, *One Hundred Proofs the World Is Not a Globe*, *The Greatest Lie on Earth*, *Cruden's Complete Concordance*, and *Irwin's Bible Commentary*, along with many other books by various authors and other online help. The Blue Letter Bible is a free app. It features two Bibles able to be read at the same time side by side and multiple other versions as well. The New King James next to the King James version shows how close the two translations are. These are older versions of the Bible, and the closer you are to the original text, the better. A quick search will find that that there are some words not found in the entirety of these Bibles.

They are:

> Planet (zero)
> Solar and Solar system (zero)
> Universe (zero)
> Space (zero) (space is used a few times with the meaning of distance between objects, not outer space)
> Sphere (zero)
> Galaxy (zero)
> Gravity (zero)
> Globe (zero)

Words that are found in these two versions of the Bible:
*World* is found 217 times in the New King James.
*Earth* is found 863 times in the New King James.
*World* is found 249 times in the King James.
*Earth* is found 906 times in the King James.

There are many words also not in the Bible, such as bible, facetime, helicopter, toothpaste, etc., but these are objects created by man (using God's resources, of course). God did not tell us everything He made; however, if He made "planets," there is no doubt that they would have received a mention, along with the earth, sun, moon, and stars, and He would have come up with better names for them.

# CHAPTER 9

---

# False Religions, the Mark of the
# Beast, and the Breadth of the Earth

*[F]or the time will come when they will not endure
sound doctrine; but after their own lusts shall they
heap to themselves teachers, having itching ears; and
they shall turn away their ears from the truth, and
shall be turned unto fables.*

*—2 Timothy 4:3–4*

God's Word says on the very first page that He gave us a protected world with the earth and water in it and also placed the sun, moon, and stars in the heavens. Yes, the heavens are right above us, unseen.

*"[T]he birds that fly in the midst of heaven"
(Revelation 19:17).*

The Bible clearly states in book 1, chapter 1, verse 1 that He made the heavens (plural) and the earth (not plural). This fact is proven all through the Bible. For example, *Judges 5:4* says "*the earth trembled and the heavens poured*". In the same first chapter of *Genesis*, in verse *17*, it says, "*God set them in the firmament of the heavens.*"

In *Genesis 1 verse 26*, the Trinity is first mentioned when the Father, Son, and Spirit say, *"Let us make man in our image,"* and then He gave man dominion over everything He had made. We are special. God made us in His image—flesh of Christ, eternal as the Father, and with a soul of the Spirit. God Himself gave us this wonderful place to thrive, build, create, and praise him. He gave us a body and a mind and a soul of our own. He gave us free will to accept Him or deny Him. Please don't take all this information the wrong way. If you or your friends and loved ones cannot overcome the lies and deceptions that Satan has perpetrated on our world concerning what our world looks like, you are not alone.

No, it will not affect your salvation. As a matter of fact, even with all the biblical and scientific proofs that have been laid out in this book, derived from God's Word and God's natural laws, very few people will be swayed. Remember a few chapters back where the great Mark Twain quote was used? That saying is so true. Worth a repeat of the great author: "It is easier to fool someone than to convince them that they have been fooled," translation: no one wants to feel stupid. We have been fooled. What the world says is in direct contradiction to what the Bible says. It's about time that we Christians stand up and back up what our Lord God says on the very first pages of His Word and His entire Bible He gave us. The "word gymnastics" that Christians play with to dance around this issue is not right. We as born-again Christians should not try to twist God's Word to incorporate a round, spinning ball into lining up with the Bible because it does not. Either the Bible is correct or it's not. Either the world is correct or it's not. We either believe it or we don't.

Words mean things.

The word *worlds* was found in my search in the King James and the New King James only twice, both in *Hebrews 1:2* where it says, *"[B]y whom also He made the worlds"* and again in chapter 11 verse 3 where it states, *"[T]hat the worlds were framed by the Word of God."* This stumped me for a moment. Could this be talking about other "planets"? Realizing what Genesis 1:1 is saying took care of this problem.

*"In the beginning God created the Heavens and the earth."* We just noted that heavens is in the plural form. The only life that we know

of is here on earth and in heaven. When you look up the definition of the word *world*, the first description given is earth. I imagine that if heaven had a dictionary and the word *world* was searched for, the first description of it would be heaven.

*"They desire better, that is a heavenly country, God has prepared a city for them" (Hebrews 11:16).*

Heaven is a real place and people and animals and life exist in worlds, not on planets that are not there. It is troubling that in other, newer versions of the Bible, the word *worlds* has been changed to universe and with blatant disregard for the ancient Greek and Hebrew in which the words were derived from. We will go into great detail about this later on. While I understand trying to reach new generations of humans by making the Bible a little easier to read, putting words in the Bible that were not there and removing words that are there is changing the Word of God to something that it was not meant to be. Bottom line is that the Bible clearly states that God Himself named the earth, the sun, the moon, and the stars. He did not name nonexistent "planets" that He did not make.

Take *John 1:1–2*. My Bible says, *"In the beginning was the Word, and the Word was with God, and the Word was God. He was in the beginning with God."* The Word is in capitals because the Word is Jesus Himself. In a Jehovah Witnesses Bible, John 1:1 has been changed to say that the Word was "a" God.

A God? Just how many gods are there?

Do we need to pray to and worship all these other gods? Of course not, but you see what happens when the words of our Holy Scriptures are manipulated. More lies abound to fit what man wants to proclaim.

There is but one truth: there is but one God. There cannot be multiple truths. Satan would have you believe otherwise. Please re-read *Revelation 22:18–19*. Woe to all the false religions of the devil's world. False religions are of the devil's making.

The Catholic church, the Mormon LDS church, Jehovah Witness, Buddhist church, Muslim church, Judaism, and any other "religion" that does not teach Jesus Christ, God's son, is the only way to God and heaven, is a lie from Satan himself.

Sorry, I'm not sorry.

"This is why the world will hate you because of me," said Jesus Himself.

*"If the world hates you, know that it hated me before you"* (John 15:18).

All other roads and religions lead straight to hell. *"No one comes to the Father but by me."* I didn't say it, Jesus Christ said it.

> *"But even if we or an angel from heaven should preach to you a gospel contrary to what we have preached to you, a curse be on him"* (Galatians 1:8).

Like everything else in this book, it's either true or its false. God Himself said it, so guess what? It is all true, and Satan is leading countless people to hell based on his false religions. These aforementioned "religions" and others are definitely false and from Satan himself. The reality of it all is that Satan is anti-god. There is coming a time soon when we humans will have to make a choice to who we will serve. It is already happening. Every prophecy has been fulfilled, and we await the coming of our Lord. When the rapture happens, man will try to explain it away with the "alien theory of abduction" that has already been "established" and planted in our brains with decades of radio and television and movies and books. The masses are already preprogrammed to believe in aliens and this false event. Even with a spiritual event like the rapture, humans left behind will not turn to God.

Mankind will be forced to receive a mark on their forehead or hands. It's already happening; people are putting chips in themselves and their animals. It will leave a mark. You will not be able to buy or sell without the mark, you will not be able to work, it will be the New World Order. The forehead and wrist are the thinnest layers of skin on the body, the required chip will be placed in one of these two locations. This has been predicted in the Bible—*Revelation 13:17, Revelation 14:11, Revelation 16:2, and Revelation 19:20.*

How scary of a time will it be when a one world government is established, and the people of earth are forced to relinquish freedoms and rights and bow to a system put into place by the devil himself. I pray God will save his people from ever having to endure this, but I believe we will see many changes and suffer much persecution for our beliefs before our Savior comes and avenges us.

*"Those who had not worshiped the beast, neither his image, neither had received his mark upon their foreheads, or on their hands; they lived and reigned with Christ" (Revelation 20:4).*

This is some deeper theology that mature Christians should know. It's scary, end-of-the-world stuff. It is not fantasy like all the space and alien movies we've talked about, it's real. The Bible is 100 percent true and accurate and has been dissected and debated for a very long time with the Bible always winning the argument, and the Bible will win the moving sun and stationary earth argument as well because truth is truth.

*"They shall turn away their ears from the truth and shall be turned unto fables" (2 Timothy 4:4).*

This is a warning. Do we want to be those fools? Do we want to keep insisting that our God made a round, spinning planet even though His word clearly says He did not? Do we want to keep worshipping the sun by placing it at the center of the "universe"? Do we want to keep teaching the same lies we were taught to our kids and grandkids? *Deuteronomy 11:18* says, *"Lay up these truths and words of Mine in your heart and in your soul, teach these truths to your children."* How many more Bible verses do we need to be convinced? The Ten Commandments teach us that we are not to worship carved images. What is a globe?

Our world worships the globe. They worship the sun. They worship Apollo (look up the hypocritic oath that new doctors have to swear on). They worship Satan. They worship anything but the real God, just like the Israelites of the Old Testament, and they saw signs and wonders that we will never see. Still they quickly fell into idol worship over and over again. God kept giving them redemption and do overs. How much longer can He stand watching what His creation is doing now? For we are far worse in the depravity of modern sin than our ancestors ever were. We just hide it better.

If we keep insisting that the earth is a spinning ball floating in outer space, then we have let Satan win. If we keep letting our kids think that the same lie is truth, we damage them just as much and heap more cognitive dissonance into their brains that they will have to fight off as adults. Again, the Christian leaders of our country must take the mantle on this issue and preach God's Word as it is, from the Bible, because it is the truth. How can any preacher preach the end times and not include these wicked lies of the devil?

*Question: How can stars fall from the sky to earth?*

*Revelation 6:13* says, *"And the stars of heaven fell unto the earth."* What are the chances that stars well past the moon (250,000 miles away) could fall through millions of miles of vacuum space onto a moving, spinning earth? Not very good chances of that happening. However, it very well could and will happen because the stars are also in the firmament, right there with the moon and sun, just like it says in Genesis, and the earth is not a moving target.

*Question: How can one tree be seen by the entire world if the world were round?*

*Daniel 4:11* says, *"The tree grew, and was strong, and it was in the midst of the earth, and the height of it reached to the heavens and could be seen to the ends of all the earth."* Is this vision factual? Or is this a lie?

*Question: Can there be an "under" to a round earth?*

*Revelation 5:3* says, *"And no one on the earth or under the earth was able to open the scroll."*

*Question: Can anyone see the entire earth while in one place if its round?*

*"The devil took Him up on an exceedingly high mountain and showed Him all the kingdoms of the world"* *(Matthew 4:8).* This ques-

tion was directed to Jesus. I'm pretty sure Jesus would have corrected Matthew as to how one should interpret what the devil showed him.

*Question: Where is heaven?*

> He is God in heaven above and on earth *below.* (Joshua 2:11)

> The smoke of the city ascended *up* to heaven. (Joshua 8:20)

> There they also sent *up* their sweet aroma. (Ezekiel 20:28)

> Their sacrifices of sweet aroma *up* to the God of heaven. (Ezra 6:10)

> The whole city going *up* in smoke to heaven. (Judges 20:40)

*Question: Which way is up on a round earth?*

*Mark 6:41* says, *"He looked up to heaven."* A compass only works on a flat plane. A compass does not point up or down. Those directions are determined by God. Heaven is up. Earth is down. Hell is below.

*Question: Are the sun, moon, and stars in a tent?*

*Psalm 19:4* says, *"The line is gone out through all the earth, and their words to the end of the world. In them He has set a tabernacle for the sun."* The word *tabernacle* is a reference for our world as to our shape. We are encased, enclosed, inside a tent-like structure.

*Question: Is all scripture from God?*

Second Timothy 3:16 says, "*All scripture* is given by inspiration of God, and it is profitable for doctrine, for reproof, for correction, and for instruction in righteousness."

*Question: When will we believe?*

John 3:12 says, "*If I have told you earthly things and you believe not, how shall you believe if I tell you of heavenly things?*"

*Question. What is the breadth of the earth?*

*Revelation 20:9* says, "*And they went up in the breadth of the earth.*" The Hebrew word for breadth is *rochaband* its meaning is this: broad, wide, not round.

God is telling us something. Are we going to listen? Repeatedly the Bible is telling us that the sun moves, that we have edges, that we have pillars, that the edges around us create a breadth, that our sun and moon are their own lights, that the stars are the only other lights in the sky and not planets. God said it, not me. This changes everything. We have been sold a bill of goods, lied to on a massive scale. What are we going to do about it? A moving sun equals no mythical gravity.

There is no bigger story anywhere about anything! This is now and has been a worldwide scam from day one, thank you Satan.

And how do you flood a spinning ball?

A simple logical question like that is laughed at. If indeed the earth was flooded like we believe from the Bible, where did all the water go? On a ball where did all the water subside to? Earlier in a previous chapter we saw the verse in Job where God says, "*Who has divided a channel for the overflowing water?*" And in verse 18 of Job 38, He asks Job, "*Have you comprehended the breadth of the ea*rth?" I admit that I had to look up the word *breadth* like a lot of those Hebrew and Greek words earlier. In Genesis 13:17, the word *breadth* is used to describe land, its length and width, not its circumference and again in 1 Kings 7. Strong's Concordance #4414 in the Hebrew defines the word *breadth* as a broad plain and width. As we remember in Isaiah, the Lord drew a circle in the deep of the seas. Like a wax seal from a king's signet on a parchment of something important, the wax was pushed down and a ring of wax on the outer edges rose up higher and created a "breadth" or walls—walls that could stop proud waves. A flat surface with outer higher walls can be flooded unlike a ball. Think about all the water that was needed to flood this earth. We have a mountain called Mount Everest that is 29,029 feet above sea level (there's that darn level thing again). In order to flood the entire world, it is obvious that the water had to be at least high enough over the top of Mount Everest so that Noah's boat had no chance of running into it. The lowest point on earth is the Dead Sea, which boarders Israel coming in at 1377 feet below sea "level." That's 30,406 feet of height in extra water covering our world. The amount of water that took is utterly astounding. If God had not devised these channels for the water to subside to, we would still be under water today. Channels do not work or even make sense on a round world. Evaporation is not an option either. Once the water finally evaporated, if it ever could, our worlds soil would be useless for millions and millions of years.

Yeah, I used millions and millions. Why not?

The other side gets away with it all the time without ever being questioned about it, and if evaporation is your answer, then why would it not keep evaporating to the point of finally being just gone? Our soil is not useless; we grow food in it daily and extract all the materials we need to build things. And the seas are not evaporating, they remain just as God wants them to remain.

The Grand Canyon is probably the greatest example we have on earth of the evidence of the flood. The Grand Canyon was a huge lake after the flood and obviously was drained quickly due to all the separating layers that are visible to the naked eye (we were "taught" that it took millions of years to create the Grand Canyon by slow erosion—more worldly crap that is taught as fact). A wall of this great lake must have broken at some point, emptying the canyon quickly. There are fossils in the Grand Canyon that could have only come from an ocean, thus proving that the world was indeed flooded. There are many other places like deserts around the world that prove the same thing with fossils being found that came from the oceans. So the world was flooded as we know from our Bible stories as kids, and that water had to go somewhere, didn't it? God tells us, just like He tells us everything else, just what He did to remove the water from the earth. This all makes perfect sense, unless we are a globe.

What else makes sense? We've talked about science, and we've talked about the Word of God a lot. The neat thing is that Gods word and science always line up together, and that makes sense. As Christians, we don't need to be afraid of the "all mighty science" as God created science. He did not, however, create science fiction.

Everything proves God as God made everything and through Him all things were made, including science.

God's math and God's laws always align perfectly. I absolutely hated math and science classes, I was a history and English and PE guy. I had to take a summer school geometry class to help me pass, but all those equations worked because they are from God. A higher intelligence was and is definitely in control of all of the mathematics that keep our lives humming along whether we realize it or not. Your natural senses that God gave you as He formed you in your mother's womb are yours and yours alone. The magical rainbows we were talking about earlier are unique to you and your vision. No one else sees them the way you do. Your smell is yours; your taste buds are yours. We do not all enjoy the same foods, do we? I love mushrooms and hate olives; my wife loves olives and hates mushrooms. If we didn't have unique senses, then we would all enjoy the same things, wouldn't we? Everyone would love mushrooms the way I do. Everyone would love the same music as I do and love all the same things as I do. That would be a pretty boring world, wouldn't it? God gave each one of us our own unique set of senses. It's okay to trust them. I'm not going to chew and swallow an olive because they are gross and that's ok for me and it's ok for you to enjoy them.

Our senses tell us when we are moving fast or slow too. I know when I'm on a roller coaster and I know when I'm stuck in LA traffic, going one mile per hour. The science world says that we are moving at over a thousand miles per hour and that we don't feel it because we are in the same atmosphere as the movement, like being in a moving car and tossing a ball in the air. The ball is moving at the same speed as the car but falls back into the hands of the thrower because the ball and car are moving at the same speed. They always use a car as the example. What about an airplane? Same thing, right? No, not right. The ball will come back down in our hands on an airplane flying through the air at three hundred miles per hour, but what about all that wind rushing over the fuselage and wings? It sure feels like we are moving faster than the atmosphere, doesn't it? Because we are. Some towering "intellect" will no doubt make some ridiculous statement like "The atmosphere outside of our system is moving even faster than our thousand-miles-per-hour earth." They are superior, do not question them.

Come on, we are not idiots. Arguments like this are just made up chalk board nonsense. Since we are on hypotheticals, try this story from the Bible. In *Joshua 10:13*, it says, *"So the sun stood still, and the moon stopped."* Okay, everyone knows that the moon rolls each night through the sky, no argument there. But the sun stopped. Let's run it back and say that they "really meant to say that the earth stopped" or "they didn't know any better back then." Now as born-again believers, we have to accept one or the other. God preformed a miracle here! We believe all the other miracles in all the other stories. Remember the beginning of this book, a bunch miracles were listed, and do you remember the statement in John where it says that *"if there were books written about all the things Christ did that, they would be so many so that the earth itself could not contain them?"* (John 21:25), and we believe them all, right? So God preformed another miracle. Updating it and telling it, the way that it should've been told is God said, "Earth, stop spinning."

Well, what happens when something spinning at a thousand miles per hour is stopped? I don't care how big the vessel is that's stopped. Stopping something moving that fast would have killed they very people God was trying to help, along with every other living thing in the world. So it's not what God said. He said what He wanted to say the way He wanted to say it because He in fact stopped the sun and not the earth. I've read esteemed pastors' commentaries about how the sun just appeared to stop, well the bible says, "so the sun stood still" so any pastor with this belief is wrong! Others make feeble attempts to hypothesize that God must have slowed the earth gradually. Always dismissing the logical and the biblical to move on to the next counter point of defending the cult of the spinning earth. Does no one ever listen anymore or does the entire population begin their rebuttal in their minds before the last sentence is spoken? Take time to digest all this information, biblical and otherwise. Let it be tossed around in your mind before you react before you dismiss.

Let God show you that His Word is true.

The world and its atmosphere are not a car or an airplane. We have winds blowing in different directions at the same time, we have balance because we have level, we sense that the sun moves because it moves, and we can see it move and we feel a strong wind that blows us in every direction. We deny our own senses given to us by God so that we can believe all the nonsense "science", that man is right and God is wrong. No one can deny the simple experiments laid out in this book because they are real science. The fact that these very simple truths can be explained by a fairly simple man must infuriate the learned educated man. What good is an IQ if you are lost in your own knowledge and can't see a loving Creator constantly at work in His creation that He made just for you!

> *"Professing to be wise, they became fools" (Romans 1:22).*

Let's not be foolish. God is not mocked, He will correct all things, and all things will be made known through Him and Him alone. We are indeed a foolish people that can be swayed into believing that our sun is still and that we move. This is just a plain and simple lie! It's from Satan, what else would you expect?

# CHAPTER 10

# No Excuse

*He that answers a matter before he hears it is a fool.*

*—Proverbs 18:13*

As I am in the middle of writing, I also have many other things going on in my life as most people do. We are very layered people, always busy with a lot on our plate. Some of us are husbands and wives and parents and grandparents and we always seem to be running around and running out of time on most days. I retired after thirty years of hard work and started a business with my son, I'm a musician, I attend a weekly Bible study with my wife, and I am very active in my church. I'm writing a book, I have a lot of books I'm always reading at any given moment, and my most favorite thing I love to do—hang out with my grandkids (seven in total now, four girls and two boys and one on the way). It tickles me each and every time I hear them call me Papa, when we get to playing too hard and they all jump on me I then become The Papa Monster. Be it Papa or Papa Monster, no one on earth loves their grandkids the way I do (I'm sure every Papa Monster thinks this). We need to be the best examples we can possibly be to our family, and that is why our family tries hard to live out the Christian life and heed the lessons from God's Word. The old saying is truer today than it was yesterday; more is caught than is taught. We are being watched and not just by our kids. When people that you work with or friends that you hang out with know that you're a Christian, you are always under the microscope. It is important to read God's Word daily to arm ourselves with the truth of God's Word and God's love. This is the only way to have shot at being the model of Christ that all of us wish to project. We want to fight the good fight and hear well done at the end of the race. *2 Timothy 4:7 "I have fought the good fight, I have finished the race, I have kept the faith"* what every Christian wants to be able to say at the end.

My wife and I were at our Bible study just last night. We meet at a friend's house with ten other couples. We are a home Bible study that joins by way of the internet with a much larger study of people at our main campus church. The topic last night was Moses and his struggles with trying to be the man and leader that God had called him to be. The pastor preaching was one of my favorites (our church is large and has more than a few pastors). I was really enjoying the message and then it happened. In the middle of his message, he stated; "man used to think that earth was the center of the universe but learned some hundreds of years ago that the sun was the center of the universe from a guy named Copernicus and that, in fact, because of the gravitational pull, the world's moved around in an orderly fashion as not to slam into each other". He tied it all together with some other point, and it all made sense to everyone. No one objected, not one, because we trust this man to speak truth.

We had twenty people in the room, and there were hundreds more at the main campus. So contrary to what the Bible says and with no proof at all, this esteemed pastor weaved into his message a false heliocentric earth and other false planets and went against all these verses laid out here.

Who can blame him? Everyone knows. It has been programmed even in Christians to believe Satan's lies! I've led a few Bible studies before and I always try to find something in a lesson to challenge people, to get them thinking in a way that maybe they had not thought of before. The Bible has wondrous true stories in it that speak to us and continue to teach us all these many years after they were written.

However, I have never led a church. What a responsibility that must be and we who are not pastors have no idea the pressure that is on them constantly. We need to continually pray for our pastors. Any time I have ever taught, it has never been to more than twenty people, but I always encourage vigorous debate and conversation, because it is in those discussions where we can truly learn and help our fellow brothers and sisters. I have never taught on this topic because I know just where the debate and conversation will go. Putting it to the written word was the only option. The idea is to let the reader make up their own mind without a screaming match of differing views where no one hears anyone. Consider this, if two people were having a serious conversation about "flat earth" and it was overheard by someone else, the probability of ridicule being injected into the dialogue rises exponentially. However, a pastor can feel free to stand behind the pulpit and pontificate about space travel, and gravity, and planets, and all things "science" with supreme confidence that no one will challenge him.

As noted, my pastor mentioned the "gravitational pull" during his message and that is exactly what happened. Was he pulled aside after the service and reprimanded about such talk? You can be sure that if he preached about what the Bible actually says about our world that he most assuredly would be confronted. In his book, *The Greatest Lie on Earth*, Edward Hendrie poses this question: If gravity existed, why would it cause both the planets to orbit the sun and people to stick to the earth? Gravity should either cause people to float in suspended circular orbits around the earth (like the "planets" do) or it should cause the earth to be pulled towards and crash into the sun.

What sort of magic is "gravity" that it can glue people's feet to the ball-earth, while causing earth itself to revolve ellipses round the sun? The two effects are very different, yet the same cause is attributed to both!

You are reading this book in what is real time to you. I have the luxury of rereading and rewriting, going back over it and adding and taking away. This very spot is one of those occasions. Because it happened again. This time. it was a Sunday morning and a different pastor preaching. He was quoting a verse that we have used here.

*Matthew 5:45*, but he changed the words. Instead of saying that *"He caused His sun to rise,"* he said, "He causes the sun to shine on the just and the unjust."

Wait, what? Slip of the tongue? Maybe. On purpose?

It clearly says that God caused the sun to rise, not to shine (although it does shine) that is not the point. The point is that this pastor changed the verse to mean something completely different, and no one was bothered by it. Words mean things. Pastors often make analogies from a Bible story and relate it back to us to make one of their good points in a story that will relate to a lot of people in their daily circumstances. I rather enjoy the analogies and stories and fun jokes and get much from them as I go to church each week to fill up on God's love and enjoy the fellowship that comes with the gathering together of fellow Christians, but can't pastors admit that some verses don't need an analogy or their personal spin or their insight? Some verses just speak for themselves such as "as the sun rose" or "the sun was told to stand still." These are not hard verses to understand; they don't need interpretation. They are not meant to be confusing; they are not similes or metaphors, they say what they say and cannot be dismissed or explained away as human error. This is God's Word, so it must be His error or we have more lies from the Bible.

During the research for this book, many other Christian and non Christian books were utilized for reference. One of the books is an in-depth study on the book of Genesis. In multiple chapters of this book, the author does the same thing my pastor did by just stating, as fact, that the heliocentric planet is obviously true and does not need to be debated.

This is a well-known book which I know many people have read and has been around a long time—1976 to be exact—but just because it's been around a while and was written by someone who started a well-known Christian institution does not make it true. There are some fine and excellent points made in this book by an obviously smart and educated man—much more so than I—but if you compare it to the Bible, a lot of the authors points go up in smoke.

As a kid, I was into music and surfing, and many other distractions like many a youth, and didn't consider the bigger questions in life. I was a preteen in the mid-1970s when this book on Genesis was written. I obviously did not read it then, but a lot of people did. This notable Christian author used a lot of big words in his book and there was indeed some interesting content in it. However, when your premise of the world that we live in has already been predetermined by mass programming and is then passed along in the written word as fact, then we have a problem—a very big problem. It does not line up with the Word of God. The author says in his introduction that the book of Genesis is the actual, factual record of real events (that's true). He also says in chapter 1 in the first sentence that Genesis is the most important book ever written. These points are agreeable. Unfortunately, fifty-five pages in, the author declares, "A cyclical light-dark arrangement clearly means that the earth was now rotating on its axis." That is simply wrong! Look over all the verses from the Bible that we have outlined so far. We went over all those verses that clearly state in our Bible that the earth does not move. He uses the word *universe* over fifty times in the first three chapters. As already noted, *universe* is a concept not found in the Bible. Additionally, he states on page 55 that God brought form and motion to the earth. Form, yes; motion, no. Again wrong! The earth does not move. On page 57, he states that the earth is indeed a planet! Wrong! Earth is earth. Planet is a *word* not used in the Bible or implied in the Bible. His further use of the words *possibly, probably, could be,* and *perhaps* permeate this book and speak for themselves. His extensive use of the terms *universe, planets, global,* and *space* also give one pause as these words and phrases are not in the Bible and are not implied in the Bible either. On page 65, he uses the term *sphere* describing the earth. Nowhere in the Bible does God call the shape of the earth a sphere. Circle, yes; sphere, no.

On the same page, he talks about the earth rotating on its axis. Where is this concept found in the Bible? It's not; the opposite is found; our earth does not move. It gets worse; in page 66, he uses the terms *earth's rotation, orbital revolution, axial wobble,* and *space curvature.* Do you think that this author was influenced by NASA, and hundreds of space movies from the 1950s, '60s, and '70s? It appears so. Page 67 is more of the same, stating that the moon only reflects the light of the sun when the Bible clearly says that the moon is its own light. And again, on page 67, he says, "This implies that the earth's axis was inclined as it is at present."

This heralded book by a well-respected Christian author is 716 pages long, and we are only up to page 67. Turning the page, we find another use of the word *sphere* where the word *earth* should have been used. The Bible is right based solely on the facts stated in the Word of God that the earth does not move and that the sun does. These things said and relayed to man by none other than the Creator Himself. The author of that book has led countless people off the deep end of a satanic round spinning earth cult by validating the world's "truths" in his book.

Jesus Himself maintained the truth of the Genesis account of creation, which was written by Moses. Jesus told the Jews that if they did not believe Moses, they would not believe him *(John 5:46–47)*. *"For if you believed Moses, you would believe me; for he wrote about me."* Moses did write about Jesus in *Genesis 3:15* and *22:18* saying, *"And I will put enmity between you and the woman, and "In your seed all the nations of the earth shall be blessed, because you have obeyed My voice."*

Do we believe that Moses was speaking of Jesus in Genesis even though He had not been born yet? Yes, we do. Did Moses get this right? Did Moses relay exactly what God wanted to be relayed in these passages? Yes, he did. But Moses got it wrong when talking about the movement of the sun? With all the compelling verses laid out so far about the motion of the sun, we can see that it is not debatable. From Genesis to Revelation, God got it right.

In the book, *The Greatest Lie on Earth*, the author makes the point that God alone stretched out the heavens and spread abroad the earth. A ball is not spread out. You spread out things, and they become flat.

*Thus saith the Lord, thy redeemer, and that he formed thee from the womb, I am the Lord that makes all things; that stretches forth the heavens alone, that spreads abroad the earth by myself. (Isaiah 44:24)*

The Christian world has done backflips and cartwheels trying to line up a spinning globe with the stationary world of the Bible. Why? The answer is obvious: what church and what pastor and what congregation wants to be labeled the "flat-earth" pastor or church? It is said that you can't mix religion and politics. What is your preferred political party? Whoa! Two of the three things that you're not supposed to talk about—faith, money, and politics. I personally have had two colleagues in my recent past dissolve their friendships with me over faith and politics. Enter at your own risk. The point is this: no matter which side you are on politically, the other side is screaming at you. Just put some news on your television set and watch. You are considered stupid by the opposite party of yours. You are accused of being ignorant for thinking the way you do. The news yells at you and push their agenda every day. They are obviously pushing and pulling for their side to win. Point is, someone is wrong!

And most don't care about proof—political, scientific, biblical, or otherwise. The earth is a round, spinning globe, and everyone knows that! Your side is wrong, and my side is right! And it's that kind of ridicule and fight apparently that the Christian church can't handle, so we cower and jump through hoops. We agree to lie against God's truth, and we are losing this battle because our own pastors and leaders can't handle the truth or they don't think it's worth the fight. Isa Blagden said that "if a lie is printed often enough it becomes a quasi-truth, and if this 'truth' is repeated often enough, it becomes an article of belief, a dogma, and men will die for it." This is what the Christian church is up against, and it needs to be aware of it and prepared to defend the word of God. The "globe" is that dogma.

To quote a great movie, "You want the truth? You can't handle the truth!" or can you?

As God told Job in chapter 38, *"Prepare yourself like a man."* This is war, and it's time to declare God's wonderful truth and to take the argument back. Make the world prove that we live on a spinning planet flying through space as we spin around at a thousand miles per hour, with a sun that is ninety-three million miles away and a rolling moon that's 250,000 miles away that we have walked on. Doesn't sound reasonable when spelled out like that, does it?

In this book a lot of questions have been asked. God's people need to take their blinders off and see the light. Question everything you've been taught, let's get our faces out of the cellphone and off Facebook. Here's a challenge for the world—put a live camera on what you say is up in "space" and film our "planet" spinning. There are some fake ones on YouTube, and guess what, they forgot the stars in the background. The stars are missing in every "real" outer space picture because constellations are very recognizable and fraud would be easy to spot so they are just left out, just like the glow of the moon. If you had a television channel that played nothing but our spinning planet all day every day, 24/7, it would be a smash hit. Heck, the potheads would watch nothing else. Watch the Tesla spin around for a few hours and decide for yourself if the footage is credible. Let's see some real pictures of upside-down buildings. Prove that water curves. Fly a plane that drops its nose every few seconds to allow for the curve until it crashes into the earth.

*"And Jesus answered him, saying, it is written, that man shall not live by bread alone, but by every word of God" (Luke 4:4).*

That verse says *every word*. God's Word all throughout the Bible, as shown here in this book, clearly and unequivocally says that the sun moves and that the earth does not! This has been shown in both the Hebrew and Greek definitions of the words used in our Bible. God is right and God wins the argument every time.

But we knew that.

So what makes a retired plumber so special that this truth would be revealed to him? Nothing—that's kind of the point. This was a question posed to me by my wife on more than one occasion. I said to her rather incredulously, "There is no way that God has 'reveled' any new truth to little old me. I am not 'Mr. Super Christian' and I am a novice of the Bible at best. Our pastors have been studying the word of God for many years. There is no way that they missed something this huge for this long." This has weighed heavily on me since God put it in my heart to expose the lies of the world and to exclaim His truth. But I can't be alone. Who else knows this and why has the lie been allowed to continue for so long?

I'm just a guy who loves the Lord and His Bible, and I happen to believe every last word in it. I believe that all scripture is from God and that all of it should be preached, taught, and defended. I believe that Christians should keep the world's lies far from our children's ears for as long as possible and train up our children in the wisdom of Gods written word. I believe that the closer your version of the Bible is to the original text, the more accurate it will be. I believe that we will be held accountable for our willful turning of our blind eyes to truth that is revealed to us through His written word. While already stated that it is not an issue that one would lose their salvation over, it is serious. By the way, you can't lose your salvation. *"I give them eternal life, and they will never perish. No one can snatch them away from me."* (*John 10:28*).

My pastors and teachers over the course of fifty years have assured me that our Bible is infallible. How can this be if they believe that we are a spinning planet? And preach it! They should know the Bible a heck of a lot better than us, so show us through scripture that the sun moving is wrong. You can't. No one can.

Every word, every verse or passage, every story and parable found in the Bible only reinforces the beliefs that God's Word is true and not confusing. The Bible has admonished us to have the faith of a child. A child's faith is strong because it has not been corrupted yet by the world. Satan has gotten everyone to believe in a lie, and it started when we were just children. That crafty serpent of old has done an outstanding job at not only fooling kids but grown adults who grew up and became pastors and teachers and leaders in our houses of worship, and it started with that graven image—that stupid globe in every school, every class, on every television set and hundreds of movies, as logos, as screensavers, in songs, in daily vernacular, on t-shirts and clothing. Indoctrination, brainwashing, and control.

It has been, and still is, an all-out assault on the Bible and the one true God who is Creator of all things. And sadly, on this issue, we, the "Christians," have lost. If you've read this book up to this point and still won't at the very least even consider these possibilities, what does that say about a job well done by Lucifer himself? Did we let him win? Is it too late? What can we do? Statistical information is fascinating and accurate. Satan lies but stats don't lie. This is just a guess, and no poll will be conducted to confirm it, but the probability of more than 5 percent of any Christians or Christian pastors reading this book, let alone the rest of the unsaved population, and believing in the truths that have been laid out in these pages is small (I hope that I am wrong about this guess). Esteemed pastors and life-long Christians will argue against these truths to the point of anger.

God wants His Holy Word and truth to be re-reviled to the born-again believing Christian, which I am and I pray you are. I know that I am saved and that I am on my way to heaven when I die. Jesus, the Creator Himself knows me and loves me. If you've been saved and accepted Jesus Christ into your heart then you too know of the blessed assurance that we have as believers. Please know that I have prayed over this topic and book more than I've ever prayed over anything in my life, except my family. I don't wish to be a fool; I wanted to know the truth above everything. God's Word has shown that truth—of that we can be sure. I have prayed to the Lord to stop me if this is wrong. "God, if you made a spinning planet and a stationary sun, please show us from your Word". I have prayed this prayer and many others like it many times over. Like many Christians, I have made mistakes in the past by kicking open doors that the Lord shut, this is not one of those times. An entire chapter could be written on all the mini miracles God ordained in the creation of *Gospel Earth*. We've had nothing but open doors and green lights. These words would have not been written if there was any doubt of the Bibles validity.

God could have made a spinning planet rotating around a non-moving sun, hurling through outer space, but He didn't. His Holy Word says what it says. He could have spared his only son from dying on a cross for our sins, but He didn't. God could have made water to curve, but He made it level. He could have stretched out the skies like a hard-molten looking glass of pink, but He made it blue, and it was good. As born-again Christians, we know from the scriptures that "*with God, all things are possible*" (*Matthew 19:26*). But we also know that God does not make mistakes. He could have made anything work the way He wanted it to work, but He doesn't go against His own natural laws, and He made things the way He made things.

So since there is undeniable truth as shown through God's Word, then what can be done to stop the world from spinning? If you have been convinced, know that you are now a very small percent of people in the world that believe in God's Word 100 percent, all of it, even the parts that say the earth does not move and the sun does. How do we overcome the lie? Is it worth the ridicule that is coming? Because it will come. It's like the political ridicule you endure if you are brave enough to speak up. Well, not entirely. With politics, you can silently vote. With this issue, we must stand up and defend God. God asks us to publicly acknowledge that we love Him when we ask Him into our hearts.

*"If you confess with your mouth, Jesus is Lord and believe in you heart that God raised Him from the dead, you will be saved" (Romans 10:9).*

It is my belief that God wants his children to stand up and publicly defend Him and His Word on this issue as well. The great commission demands that we go into the world to preach and teach His Word. *"Go into all the world and preach the gospel to all creation" (Mark 16:15).* How will they know if no one tells them? This issue is only less important than that one. But it's real important—heck, it's mind-blowing. Can you imagine the chaos in our world that would occur by the revelation that all of humanity has been lied to and that we all fell for it? Governments would crash, the world's economy would suffer, cats and dogs living together, mass hysteria (a little Ghostbusters humor). If you turned on your evening news and every news anchor on every station was talking about how we have been lied to, the earth does not move and the sun does, that we never went to the moon and that we live in a protected environment, and that of all of this information lines up with the Christian Bible that has been sitting on our bookshelves for all these years and it's all backed up with real pictures and video and scientific experiments and math verifies it as well, millions and millions of people would believe and be saved from an eternity of suffering in hell without the love of Jesus. So yes, it's worth the fight.

*"let God be true, and everyman a liar" (Romans 3:4).*

Pastors, I love you all dearly. I respect you tremendously. Do the right thing and speak out to your congregations. Preach truth. Do not let the world sway you into lies and destruction. Reform is coming. The day of the Lord will soon be at hand, and I pray He is not disappointed about the lies we've allowed to become truth in our minds and in our churches. We have time to right this wrong but with the way the world is going at present moment, it may not be much longer.

# CHAPTER 11

# Lying Lucifer

*Ye are of your father the devil, and the lusts of your father ye will do. He was a murderer from the beginning, and abodes not in the truth, because there is no truth in him. When he speaks, he lies, for he is a liar and the father of lies.*

—*John 8:44*

Have you ever been lied to? Of course you have, lying has been around a long time and we have all done it, and if we think that we haven't then we are lying to ourselves which is problematic on many levels. When you lie or you are lied about, know that lying is an invention and tool of "the father of lies," the devil himself. Lies have ended marriages, friendships, and even lives. Please don't let lies keep you from a deeper love and truth that God has spelled out for you in His Word. A stationary sun is a lie from Satan and it contradicts the Bible.

Lucifer and his minions will do and have done anything and everything to keep you away from the loving arms of the Creator and the truths that only He can impart to us. The devil knows his time is short, and he gets more desperate with every passing day. The world seems to be getting worse day by day because, well, it is getting worse. With every new invention or mode of new entertainment we come up with, the devil looks for a way to corrupt it. He has tainted almost every good thing that man has ever invented. God is the one who placed all the materials in the ground and oceans for His creation to find and utilize, and mankind has done a most wondrous job of creating the intricate devices that make our everyday life better—cars, trains, planes, phones, film, computers, indoor plumbing. We take all of it for granted, especially in America. However old the earth is, for most of its history, we did not have these comforts. Most of these things have only come about in the last one hundred years or so, but we don't remember life without these things and all we want is more.

Yes, we are smart, and we have all of these comforts, but we are still depraved without the guidance of the Holy Spirit—the same Holy Spirit that guided the authors to write the words of the Bible. We have taken nearly every invention and comfort made for us and twisted it to a dark place that has damaged us to degrees we can't even fathom. This happened because we bought the lies of the devil when we could have had the grace and protection of the truth. We alone have control over what decisions we make; we can control our thoughts; we can control our reaction to anything that comes our way. We can make our own decisions and we can and we should and we must stand up for the Word of God. And, we need to be able to recognize subtle and obvious lies that are in front of our eyes daily so we can one, be aware of them and two, make choices and decisions based on truth.

Think about this: is there anything that would cause you to receive the mark of the beast? Let's look at this hypothetical.

The end times are here, the New World Order is being put into place, a false peace will be abundant, but it will come with a price. You won't be able to buy or sell without the new required chip implanted in you. You can't work without it either. It is mandatory, it replaces money and credit cards and driver's license, passports, and all forms of identification. Moreover, the attack on Christianity has escalated. It is outlawed because it is seen as intolerant. It is against the law to be a Christian now even in America. They preach against homosexuality, they preach that Jesus is the only way to heaven, they believe that the sun moves and the earth does not. Does this sound too farfetched? It is not, this has been happening in other countries for years. Now imagine that your child or your grandchild is starving or threatened with death if you do not receive the mark. What would you do? I'm not quite sure which is right—pre-tribulation, mid-tribulation, or post-tribulation. I'm hoping for pre-tribulation, but there is good argument for all three which will not be argued or debated here.

But when the rapture happens. it is sure to cause chaos. Have you ever wondered why America isn't mentioned in the Bible in the end times? The stats show that 65 percent of Americans believe in God. That's not a bad number, I hope that's true. Now if 65 percent of Americans disappear—and mind you, these are supposed to be the good and moral people—who's left and what happens next?

Have we resolved in our hearts to die for our faith? Fear not those who can only kill the body and not the soul. The body is temporary, the soul is eternal. We have all lost loved ones due to death. The stats are amazing. One out of every one person will die (unless raptured). I have loved ones in heaven that I can't wait to be reunited with. Oh, the sheer joy of seeing them again and to live forever with the one who loves me most. I can hardly imagine, and I can't wait. Our goal should be to know that God is real, that His Word is real. Know what is coming and be prepared. We have to be educated enough that we can spot the lies quickly. This outrageous lie of a spinning world has been going on for hundreds of years. The father of lies has corrupted everything in this world, including trying to corrupt they very Word of God. Examples to follow in chapters ahead.

There is an old song from 1969 that really scared me as a kid. It probably scared you too if you are old enough to remember it. Below the words are listed for you. As you read them and maybe sing along as you remember the tune, think back if you're old enough to remember how we were living as Christians back then. Our church in Huntington Beach, California was in the middle of the "Jesus Revolution". Can you remember the vibe? Do you remember the praise music? Very cool, very '70s. We were ready for the second coming of our Lord. We praised Him, we shouted, we danced, we longed for our Savior. Guess what, He is still on the way. But where is that urgency today? We need to be aware, we need to be ready, because He is still coming and He will come like a thief in the night, and no one knows the date or time. We are closer than we've have ever been.

> Life was filled with guns and war
> And everyone got trampled on the floor
> I wish we'd all been ready
> Children died; the days grew cold
> A piece of bread could buy a bag of gold
> I wish we'd all been ready
> There's no time to change your mind
> The Son has come, and you've been left behind.
> A man and wife asleep in bed
> She hears a noise and turns her head, he's gone
> I wish we'd all been ready
> Two men walking up a hill
> One disappears and one's left standing still
> I wish we'd all been ready
> There's no time to change your mind
> The Son has come, and you've been left behind
> There's no time to change your mind
> How could you have been so blind
> The Father spoke, the demons dined
> The Son has come, and you've been left behind.
> ("I Wish We'd All Been Ready" by L. Norman, 1969)

The sermon that was never preached—it doesn't need to be preached because everybody just automatically knows that the earth is round and moving. A lie believed.

What's needed is for preachers to unite and preach with conviction that the Bible got it right, God got it right, or tell us that these are mistakes and God didn't really mean what He said. It is no wonder that the Bible issues a warning to be careful to want to be teachers, leaders, and pastors; they are held to higher standards and will be held in accountability for their dissemination of Gods truths to His people. This will be the hardest thing that men of God have ever had to do. You know the truth, let it set us free.

*Gospel Earths* message is one of hope, that through the conversations that are sure to ensue, we will all grow in our faith and our eyes will be eyes that see the obvious words of God. And they were sitting there in plain sight.

Other things are in plain sight too. Like the sexual images pushed on us for so long and so often that our tolerance levels move. It slowly creep in on us just like the sin that it is and nobody notices. Remember back when a Rated-R movie was taboo? Most people today probably don't remember that, but not too long ago around the 1960s things got a little racier in the movies. Now you could go pay to see in the cover of darkness things that were meant to be seen only between one man and one woman. With Satan at work, now in the year 2020, R-rated is okay for an impressionable teenager to see. Now today, even porn in our homes is not uncommon, forget R-rated. As already mentioned, I don't like sitting down wasting time in front of a television and my wife can only drag me to a movie about once a year. However, I have to acquiesce more often than I'd like to admit and watch a show with her, usually on Friday nights (date nite). She enjoys cheesy horror movies and I get to be the one who holds the remote to fast forward through the sex scenes. We are no prudes but we have found that by me showing respect to my wife because she is not fond of me looking at other women, she in turn is very attracted to me for doing that for her. It's a win win. Granted we have been married a long time and two people who are committed to each other go through years of training together so some success is to be expected. So friends and family know what we do on date nite and also are aware of my resistance to enjoying movies. So we get lots of recommendations of shows we should watch. Not too long-ago some friends were insisting that we give "Game of Thrones" a chance. It's amazing, you'll love it, etc. So against better judgement we put on episode one. This was a mistake for us, the show wasn't five minutes old and there is a sex scene involving a midget and more than a few naked women. Porn is not the shameful thing it used to be, its accepted. You don't have to sneak out to see it at a dirty theater anymore, you don't have rental stores anymore, it graduated to in-home theater and is now on demand right in front of our computers. This very same computer that this book was written on can have anything you want on it in two seconds just like yours. And where did it all start? What generation decided that we could let sin creep into the public view for the price of admission? Today it's free. Porn has been around since the invention of the camera so we can do some simple math from the date of the first cameras and watch the timeline of our societal breakdown of decency from that point to today. The general population had the use of cameras by the early 1900s and by the 1920s there was an abundance of pornography in all the latest forms. In 1933 the first female to bare all on the big screen was legendary actress Hedy Lamarr in the film Ecstasy. While the nude scene was scrapped and never saw the light of day, a wicked wheel was set in motion. It took only a few more years before Jane Mansfield became the first major American actress to bare all on screen in the early sixties. The insatiable sexual appetite of man has demanded a progression of sin because there is a market for it. A huge market. If there were no market for it then porn would have died out like Disco. Instead it metastasized, taking debase to new levels because again, there is a market for it. Breaking free from any addiction be it drugs, alcohol, sex, or a flawed belief system is a must for our society if we are to have a fighting chance of saving our country from further consequences. This may have started long ago but our generation of the here and now is just as responsible as past generations, maybe even more so. We keep passing the sin down the line. We need a new generation of "Jesus Freaks" to rise up and start a revolution based on Gods truths.

Not wishing to instill paranoia into anyone, but if you don't think that anything that anyone has ever done, said, viewed, or participated with on the internet is not recorded, then you are a darn fool. There is nothing that is done in secret that will not be made known, and God doesn't like secrets.

*For God will bring every work into judgement, including every secret thing, whether good or evil. (Ecclesiastes 12:14)*

*"Can anyone hide himself in secret places, so I shall not see him? Says the Lord "do I not fill heaven and earth?" says the Lord. (Jeremiah 23:24)*

*There is no secret that can be hidden from you! (Ezekiel 28:3)*

*Your charitable deeds done in secret, your Father who sees in secret will Himself reward you openly"* (Matthew 6:4) *(*This is a good secret.*)*

*I will utter things kept in secret from the foundation of the world* that's a good one, we got a secret and the foundation of the world in the same verse. *(Matthew 13:35)*

*There is nothing hidden which will not be revealed, nor has anything been kept secret but that it should come to light. (Mark 4:22)*

*For nothing is secret that will not be revealed, nor anything hidden that will not be known and come to light. (Luke 8:17)*

These are scary verses.

Lucifer, once a beautiful majestic part of the heavenly host, was overcome by pride, jealousy, and lust. He does not sleep. He does not feel sorry for the weak or the lost. He thrives on making sure that others suffer with him. He can't see you the way God sees you but he notices all our weaknesses by merely watching us, and by watching us he knows some of our secrets too. He is a manipulator, a deceiver, and a liar. He deserves no praise; he deserves no glory. Yet, we choose to give it to him through worshiping, falsely, the lies he has woven into our hearts and minds about a host of issues. He helps us to sin and then uses our sin against us. Cast him out this day!

# CHAPTER 12

## End Times

*Blessed is he that reads, and they shall hear the words of this prophecy, and keep those things which are written for the time is at hand.*

*—Revelation 1:3*

I don't advocate violence. Christ the Lord did not advocate violence, and we should seek to model a life after Him. "*Turn the other cheek and do unto others as you would have them do unto you*". (*Matthew 5:39)* It is the world that we will have to contend with that will turn violent. The world has shown a propensity toward violence since its inception. Look at the political fights happening today over who the president should be. American Christian, realize that we have it so good in America. For now, we can still worship and pray and live life normally.

Times are good as of this writing, the unemployment levels are historically low, and consumer confidence is high. We all want to watch our kids and grandkids grow up in a safe world and do well. The economy is good enough that we were able to start our own business and, with God's support and guidance, watch it grow. I have no doubt, however, that this will not last. I don't like being this right about something like this, but things have just changed. The coronavirus is upon us, the actual date today is April 18, 2020, and it's

3:30 a.m. in California. This paragraph was obviously written before our worldwide pandemic. Notice I didn't say "global pandemic." The end times are coming and in fact are here. Oh geez, this dude is a doom's day guy too! Hey, once again it's not me, and look around… turn the news on for a minute. It feels like it's going down out there. We should not be surprised, it's in the Bible and we are witnessing the "end times" right now. There is coming a day when brother will be against brother. I don't want to sound like those crazy guys on the corner with the big red signs warning of the end, but it is coming.

> *"Do not think that I came to bring peace on earth. I did not come to bring peace but a sword. For I have come to 'set a man against his father, a daughter against her mother, and a daughter-in-law against her mother-in-law'; and 'a man's enemies will be those of his own household'" (Matthew 10:34-35).*
> Jesus the Christ.

A sobering verse that we would all do well to digest.

Another not so friendly verse the church should consider,

> *"So, because you are lukewarm, and neither hot nor cold, I am going to vomit you out of my mouth" (Revelation 3:16).*

The message of that verse is not good. This was a church Jesus is talking about. We are the church. Wherever you are and wherever you live, the churches we attend weekly and the ones we visit, we say that "we are the church." This church that Jesus was talking about thought that they were doing good. The church of Laodicean had been blessed by God with material wealth and apparently thought that they were doing great and in need of nothing. They became haughty and proud of their wealth and apparently lost sight of what was important and just who it was that had allowed them to accumulate such wealth. Deep down, are not some of us just like that?

And some of our churches are like that too. God still loved that church and says that He only rebukes those that He loves. Are we too comfortable to notice that we are also being rebuked? In verse *20* of *Revelation 3*, God still gives that church a way out. He says to *"repent, that He stands at the door and knocks"*. He is still knocking, calling us out to be "zealous," to overcome the world. Well, here's that opportunity.

The devil has always had limited power but Satan was given the authority to offer Jesus the world. *Matthew 4:8*. He still has that power today and uses it as he wants. He is still free to give to those who want what he has to offer. Look at Hollywood; it is obvious that the devil has his hands in everything, and it is absolutely criminal to allow our children to see what they have access to see at any moment at any time of day at the click of a button. Talk about programming. "Lord Father God, forgive us as a people for letting that kind of sexual sin into the lives of our sons and daughters"—and we didn't have a leg to stand on because we looked too. The money that the sex industry has made off of the human race would rival any form of money exchange of any kind for all time. I have a passion for any human who has had to battle an addiction of one kind or another, they are powerful and hard to break free from. Everyone has a past and I am no different in that area. I am no saint, I have sinned, and I am a sinner. I have hurt the ones I love as a result of my sins. I am ashamed of my sins and should have protected and guarded myself from sin better so that my witness for the Lord would be better received. But we are all sinners and all fall short and we are in need of a Savior, and if we would all humble ourselves to the Lord we would see that, like Paul, we are all chief sinners and no one can cast the first stone.

I am forgiven however, and have accepted my Lord's forgiveness. You too are forgiven if you have asked for forgiveness. Remember, we have not because we ask not (*James 4:2*). That works for forgiveness of our sins better than any other request. We as the Christian body need daily help and guidance from the Holy Spirit, and we need to pray daily for ourselves and the church of our Lord Jesus Christ. Accountability is needed. My lovely and gracious wife of thirty-three years can walk into my office and look at my computer anytime she wants too. My iPad and phone are hers as well. She has all the passwords. Whatever your sin is, now is the time to deal with it because the days are getting shorter.

God through His forgiveness makes us all brand new, but like a loving Father who has to discipline his child for repeat offenses, the Lord will only take so much. Don't be fooled, if you have a pet sin that you try to keep hidden. Remember this: "*Nothing is covered that won't be uncovered, and nothing hidden that won't be made known*" (*Matthew 10:26*). An Almighty God is watching us, and unlike a fake Santa, he is real, and our lives have real consequences for our actions. What action is required of the church in regard to what the Bible has to say about our creation? If it is not yet obvious this far into this book that God's Holy Word is being misrepresented on the grandest of scales, then maybe no action is required at all. Close this book, close your Bible and let's just close our eyes and ears to the truth. Maybe the world is a round, spinning globe, and the Bible has lied to us or at best deceived us. Whoa, that is blasphemy to a Christians ears! Well God gave us His Word to study, to hide in our hearts, to love, so that is just what we have to do. We have to know the Word of God. It is perfect, and we base our entire Christian faith on it. Do you think that God has instructed us to hide "memorize" scripture in our hearts if it's all wrong? Now the verses listed about the movement of the sun are not the typical verses one memorizes, but you see the point, don't you? *All* scripture is good to hide in our hearts, so the words were and are correct and good for us to memorize because they are *all* true. God does not deceive, He does not confuse, He is the author of all. No way is His Holy Word compromised. If we seek the truth, the truth will be revealed to us. *"You will know the truth, and the truth will set you free" (John 8:32)*. How about this verse from *Romans 1:25 "They exchanged the truth of God for a lie and worshiped and served what has been created instead of the Creator."*

The globe was created by man, and the world was created by God.

Oh, that we as the church of Jesus Christ would not be luke-warm. It says in *Galatians 4:16, "Have I become your enemy because I told you the truth?"*

I am not your enemy; I am not the church's enemy. I love the Lord and I love His church and I love His Word. I've said many times thus far, that it is going to be hard to overcome this deception and if these words before you and the Bible passages that our pastors teach from every Sunday are not enough to convince, then prayer is what we have left. And prayer works. If you are a born-again believer and trying your best to live a godly life in this messed up world, and you pray on a consistent basis, then I know that you have seen the power of prayer work in your own life. I am praying for you and our churches and our pastors and our nation and our world. Truth is usually obvious; black is black, good is good, and evil is evil. Two plus two is four, and our Bible is not full of errors. The sun moves.

The Bible is the key to all of this. It's either right or its wrong. We don't get to assume or interpret anything written is saying something other than what it is saying. To suggest that Matthew knew nothing about the movement of the sun is ridiculous. The followers of Christ knew better than any humans who ever lived the power of God Himself. And they knew the word. They would have known the story of how God stood the sun still.

> *And the sun stood still, and the moon stayed, until the people had avenged themselves upon their enemies. Is this not also written in the book of Jasher? So, the sun stood still in the midst of heaven, and hasted not to go down about a whole day. (Joshua 10:13)*

There is a lot in that verse, and Matthew was well aware of the sun's movement and the stopping of the sun, a miracle of God. *"He makes His sun rise on the evil and on the good" Matthew 5:45*

Also notice that the sun stood still in the midst of heaven. The sun is right above us, and heaven is right above us. And Matthew would also know about the book of Jasher. What is the book of Jasher and why is it not in our Bible? When you look up the book of Jasher on the internet, the first commentary you'll read is that this book was written much later than biblical times. Wrong! More lies of Satan and the world because here it is (the book of Jasher) mentioned in the book of Joshua of the Old Testament written over three thousand years ago.

The book of Jasher, in my opinion, should be included in the Bible. It is 91 chapters of historical overview of the entire Old Testament and I found no conflicts with our canonized Bible of today. In fact, it is a historically factual book that confirms everything in our Bible and has some very interesting details that make sense when read in conjunction with the Holy Scriptures. God said don't remove or add to His Word. Should this book be included in the Bible or should it not be? Was this book removed, or would we now be adding to it by placing it in the holy scriptures? Matthew knew of it, and when he quoted Jesus saying that the *"sun rises and sets on the just and unjust,"* he also knew that the sun moved.

These are not the Bible days and I don't consider myself as being anything special or anyone who is special but God has given me these words, they are not mine. They are from the Lord. It is His words, His finger on the wall, His Spirit guiding mine. If I ignored the call of God then I would be in danger of being found as one who was lacking.

I must drive the point home that I am no super Christian. As a matter of fact, I am just a normal Christian who answered a call from the Lord. I felt the Holy Spirit wake me up, usually around three most mornings (sometimes even earlier) to go down to my office and write. I like to sleep just like everyone else, but the call was strong. My wife would come down hours later and wonder in amazement at what was going on. She is very sensitive to the Spirit of God and has been praying fervently that doors would be shut if that was what was needed. I have learned over the years to trust her godly senses. If she said no, then you would not be reading this. He who finds a good wife has found a very good thing. We have witnessed what closed doors look like and, because of trial and error, would never kick another closed door open. The consequences are too great. During the incarnation of this book to date, we have encountered only open doors. God be praised! But know this: all I wanted at the inception of this endeavor was to know the truth. Had the truth proven that the Bible was wrong, then I would have made that known too.

Many pastors will disagree with what I am trying to do. I can hear it now behind closed doors: "Even if we agree with you, we cannot and will not become the church of the flat earthers." The evening news will mock, the newspapers will mock—it's already being mocked on the internet. A database will be compiled as to know where the Bible-believing Christians live and which ones have guns and which ones are the crazy ones who believe that the sun moves. The normal Christians may be left alone, I don't know, but the ones that believe 100 percent in God's Word and will not deny it will be tracked. "They" already track us and know what we buy, how we shop, and what we drive. "They" know our credit score and how much money we make. "They" scan our driver's licenses and get more information on us than we know about us, and soon we will be required to have an information chip planted inside of our bodies. I am not a conspiracy nut. This stuff is real. These are the end times. It is predicted in the Bible and is happening today. Will we put our collective Christian heads in the sand? Nineteen eighty-four has finally shown up. We are here. The fight is real. The question is, are we up for it as born-again believers? George Orwell (Eric Blair) wrote *1984* long before the 1980s, and while he may have gotten the decade wrong, his words ring truer today than ever before. "The truth is a revolutionary act in times of universal deceit." Another quote from the masterpiece *1984*: "Being in a minority of one did not make you mad. There was truth and untruth, and if you clung to the truth even against the whole world, you were not mad." Brothers and sisters in Christ, we are being controlled by the "thought police." In an all to realistic way, "Big Brother" is real. His name is Satan. If the sun moves, then "gravity" falls apart, and no one can explain gravity because it is not real. When you're done laughing at this thought, try to explain it to yourself. You can bet that Satan is laughing.

We who are privileged enough to get to live in America don't realize what we have. The whole world was made by God and is constantly being protected by what God made, but not all is equal in the world. America is the lone superpower. We who live here have access to the very best of everything. We have the best doctors, the best roads, the best schools. We have freedom—freedom that so many before us fought for so that we might have all these things. Most of the rest of the world is not as fortunate as we are, and Christians in other countries are being killed for their faith. This fact is not often reported on by our news today, but it does sneak into the news cycle every once in a while. These attacks and deaths happen on a daily basis. Imagine living in a country where you can be put to death for your thoughts and beliefs. That's real, and its coming to our neighborhood sooner than we would like to think.

You have a nice car, you have a good job, maybe a house that has your name on the paperwork, and a couple of kids. Your biggest worry is picking your children up from baseball or dance, or piano lessons, etc. We got it pretty easy. Even the poorest of us in America usually don't go to sleep hungry. It can be gone in very short order. Most of the history of mankind over time has been violent. God wiped us out almost completely for all the violence we perpetrated on this earth at one point. History will repeat itself. No, God will not ever flood the earth again, but we will turn on each other because we are wicked and sinful. I feel compelled to at least mention this Corona Virus thing as it all ties together with everything else surrounding our world. The control of those at the top of the worldly food chain have shown that they can and will do anything to own the minds of the masses. You can guess what my views are on this, but they will have to wait for a sequel.

Attention all atheist and non-believers: do contradictions exist in the Bible? As born-again Christians, we are taught that God's Word is infallible, that there are no contradictions. I have always believed this and still do, but what has been done here? *Gospel Earth* has given the world, atheists, and non-believers exactly what they've been looking for since the Bible was written. Here it is, the Bible is indeed wrong because it says that our sun moves and the earth does not. There you go, Mr. and Mrs. Atheist. Have at it. Force the Christian church to defend God's Word. It is what this book is all about, what it was meant to do. If the church caves on this issue, then shame on us. Regardless of all the verses that have been laid out here and all the meanings of the words used in the Hebrew and the Greek showing them to be true and correct, the church will do more "verbal gymnastics" and agree with the world that our sun is stationary and that the earth spins, if only to not be labeled the "flat-earth Christians."

We should own what the Bible says and own what our Creator said in the very first book ever written. We are at a crossroads of right and wrong, of Satan versus God, and time is running out. The Bible says, *"Narrow is the gate and difficult is the way which leads to life, and there are few who find it" (Matthew 7:14).*

This is one of those narrow gates. Do we have what it takes to enter through it? If we can't defend God, why should He defend us? The Bible also says that *"if we confess our sins He is faithful and just to forgive us of our sins and to cleanse us from all unrighteousness" (1 John 1:9).* But if we deny Him, He will also deny us. *"If we endure, we will also reign with him. If we disown him, he will also disown us." (2 Timothy 2:12).* Again, denying the Lord's creation is denying Him in my opinion, and what good is writing a book if you can't have your own opinion.

It's hard to understand how we born-again believers can accept all the other miracles and yet deny the miracle of this amazing earth God has made for us. We should give thanks every single day to Him for protecting us from the "waters above." Just because He promised that He would not flood the world ever again doesn't mean that we should not be appreciative of that fact. He is in a constant state of keeping mankind safe while at the same time giving us all that we need to survive here.

If something is worth keeping, it's worth fighting for too, and the other side feels the same way. They may know it's all false, but they will die defending the right to call God a liar in regard to the creation argument. The globe is their dogma and they are willing to die for it. What about us? Are we ready? Are we ready to die? The

Christian church has been under siege since basically forever, and it's high time we fought back. I don't know what's going to happen, but I know that it's going to be okay because God knows best and is working things out exactly how He intends too at every moment of every day. Life could come down crashing around me (maybe because of this book), I don't know, but I know that He is guiding me through it, and everything that happens from here on out is in His hands. I'm realizing that it always has been, and feeling foolish for ever thinking anything different. Life may come crashing down around you as well at some point. Try to remember when it does to pray first and react second. We are instructed to praise God always, even in the storms. Especially in the storms.

> *Forgive me, Father, and thank you for loving a sinner like me. I cannot wait to see you face to face. I imagine asking Paul and George as they greet me at the door to take me by the hand. Help me understand. Michael, wield that mighty sword. Hey, Gabriel. Gabriel, blow that horn of yours. Hey, Nana, Peter, James, and Paul, Matthew, Mark, and Luke. Mary. Hey, John, I'm going to see the king. Hey, David, I'm going to see the king. Hey, Rahab, I'm going to see the king. Hey, Thomas, there ain't no doubt no more, is there? Holy Maker, in reverence I fall down. Oh, Spirit, Father three in one, and Jesus, you took my place, you saved the human race. Thank you, God.*

It was late at night when I walked away from penning that prayer and came back to writing a day later. My intent was to delete it, I changed my mind. The prayer was about me thinking what my first moments in heaven would be like. I figured that the Apostle Paul probably gets the best seats in the house when a sinner comes home, and with me coming through the gates, I know that my dad George would be talking Paul's ears off waiting to welcome me. George Halley is actually my father-in-law, but he was the best example of a dad as I have ever known and a fine pastor. I'd see Michel and Gabriel and all the great men and women of Bible stories, then fall at the feet of Jesus in eternal gratitude. It is my most sincere concern for those who don't know Jesus that they would come to a salvation knowledge of Him whether you believe these words or not. He made the world for you, He gave you life and breath, He loves you, and He wants you to spend eternity with Him. This is mind-blowing stuff. If you are a Christian and you don't belong to a Bible-teaching Bible-believing church, go find one. Join and get involved with other God-loving people. We are going to need each other. We can overcome, we can take the heat and the insults that are on the way, but we need to hold to what God has said.

Since the end times are obviously in front of us let's do some more hypotheticals. Imagine if this were the criteria for life or death; You know that Gods word is true, but you are forced to answer one question, "does the sun move"? Your answer of yes means death, answer no and you and your loved ones live. What would you say? Two plus two is four, you know it to your core, just as I believe God's Word and know to my core that in fact the sun does move. Just like an Orwellian novel, things are getting weird, getting scary, and things are going to change. A lot of people will be too distracted to even notice. Two plus two is five. Look at abortion. We American Christians are not having a very big impact in reversing this terrible and ugly spot on our legacy regarding that, are we?

Has the other side won? Do we now love "Big Brother" instead of God? We got rid of slavery because it was morally wrong. Why is the murder of a living child in the womb not morally wrong? It is! Will we ever be able to move the needle on these issues, or is all lost?

It appears that they have won the stationary sun battle. Look at this, an entire book had to be written just to open the eyes of the already born-again believers who should have known this fact a long time ago. Had we done due diligence over the years, this topic would be a non-topic. Everybody would just know that the sun moves, and the earth does not move, but we believe the opposite. Slowly, over time, the devil weaves his ugliness into our world until something is just normal and accepted that didn't used to be normal or accepted. We in America don't live with what Christians in other countries live with daily—abuse, torture, loss of life. It's real, and it will be here in America sooner than later. We are on the slope and it indeed is slippery. The red pill has been swallowed, the matrix is real. Can is open, and worms are everywhere.

There are many Christians who seek, by one way or another, to compromise Scripture with the assumed evolutionary history of the earth. No doubt that good, well-intentioned men and women of faith have at one time or another promoted these various ideas, trying to reconcile what the world believes with what the Bible says. As previously noted, I have personally heard from the pulpit out of the mouth of my own pastor that gravity (which is a theory) is indeed fact and that there are indeed other "planets" swirling around an immovable sun just like us, just like our earth—even though the Bible contradicts these statements. They are never challenged; it's just taken as fact because "everybody knows that's how it is." We sit there in the pews and take it Sunday after Sunday. No one wants to rock the boat.

Well, the boat is rocking and filling up with the truth. God has a life jacket for us called the Bible. It will save you; it will set you free, it will bring you to a deeper understanding of God and all His majesty. Take this book to your pastor and ask him to explain to you just how the earth moves and how the sun does not based on the Bible that he preaches out of every Sunday. If you are a student at any level in your education, make a teacher prove to you that water curves over the round earth and that it is not really level. If you are a born-again believer and a mother or father, discuss and debate with your children around the dinner table about this topic. Take them to a beach or a large lake and do your own scientific experiments with them. Don't let the public-school system with their agenda indoctrinate your kids and grandkids. Where do the facts take us? How do those facts line up with the Bible? If you are a man or woman of influence of any kind, use your influence for God and His Word.

This issue must be forced out into the open, and Christian men and women of influence need to be the ones to take it up and bear your cross. God's Word has been lied about. What are we as Christians going to do about it? If indeed we are a nation of Christians (65 percent), then we are the majority, yet we have let the louder minority run us over and force evolution and space and aliens and planets and all kinds of perversions down our throats, and we sit back and take it. It's time to say, "No more lies." It's time for the truth. The truth is indeed out there, and His name is Jesus.

The world will not relent. The onslaught against our Bible will continue until the day of Christ's return. It does not change the fact that they are wrong, and God is right and true. It doesn't mean that we shouldn't try. We should be the ones to hold firm and not relent.

The Bible says:

Jesus died on the cross, was dead for three days, and rose again.

The Bible says Jesus was born of a virgin,

The Bible says Jesus caused the blind to see and the lame to walk.

The Bible says sex is to be between a man and woman only in marriage.

The Bible says there is an end to our earth.

The Bible says our sky is a hard-polished looking glass.

The Bible says we should study His Word and know what it says.

The Bible says God created.

The Bible says the sun moves.

The Bible says the earth will not move.

Do we get to just choose what parts of the Bible we will believe in, which stories are true, and what stories will we dismiss because we just know that they can't be true? Something so fundamental as the shape of our world and the moving of our sun and the nonmovement of our earth is clearly spelled out in God's written word yet we have turned our back on it in the face of so called "science." How long have we gone to church? How many messages have we heard about a moving sun? Maybe you were raised in the church from childhood or maybe you're a new believer just trying to figure things out for yourself. Wherever we are in our walk with the Lord, we all hear the sermons on Sundays about all these miracles and all the other stories in the Bible, and we believe in them, but we refuse to accept that Satan has craftily and cunningly caused doubt in God's Word by twisting the facts from "the sun moves and the earth does not" to "the earth moves and the sun does not."

It's not surprising that the world fell for it, but I am disappointed that in fifty-plus years of faithful church attendance by me and my family at Bible-believing and Bible-teaching churches, that this huge deception was gotten away with for so long without us hearing one sermon on it, apparently passed over by every preacher in every major church in America and all the small ones too. What side will you be on when you are asked that one question? Do we have what it takes to stand for God and His Word? Will we be strong when we are faced with being forced to have a chip implanted into us? It is fairly obvious that life has changed for us recently and the Bible tells us what is coming. It will only get worse and it will never get better until we are with our Savior for all time.

# CHAPTER 13

## Spirit Led

*If I have told you of earthly things and you believe
not, how shall you believe if I tell you of heavenly
things?*

—*John 3:12*

My wife has been constantly questioning me as this book was
being put together. She said just this morning on our daily
walk, "What if you're wrong?" she knows the Bible and accepts the
truths laid out in *Gospel Earth*, but her role in all of this was to vali-
date Gods truth and keep me honest. As a pastor's kid she knows the
Bible well and did a good job.

I told her, "If I'm wrong, that means God is wrong, and He is
not wrong." I didn't write the Bible, I just read it.

What every Christian needs most besides Jesus in their hearts is
daily time in His Word. I didn't read the Bible the way that I should
have for many years of my going to church, professing to be a good
Christian. I was not. I took my Bible with me to church, and I would
study a lesson to be prepared for a Bible study, but I did not have an
insatiable appetite for it. Once I got obvious sin out of my life and
really started getting into the Word of God, that's when the Lord
really started moving in my life. I was ignorant to the fact that He
really is our heavenly Father and that He is always watching us, always

wanting to help us. That is scary to think about. A Being named God has been constantly watching me since the day I was born, He saw all my sins and still loved me. God is not obligated to make life easy for us or to be our personal genie. He does, however, have many attributes—friend, savior, guiding light, teacher, comforter, forgiver, and many more. But the first, or maybe second, way He is able to guide us is through His Word. He gave us a way to know Him on a deep and intimate level, but He won't force us to read it. The Bible can seem big and daunting and intimidating, but it really is not.

The stories are inspiring and instructing and alive. We are told that if we read His Word that we will be blessed. So let's read it. Get to know God through it. Pray for knowledge, pray for wisdom, pray that as you get to know the Lord more through it that He will reveal Himself to you and show you His purpose for your life. After all, isn't that what we all want—to know why we are here, what the meaning of our life is? Your answers about your personal experience and your meaning in life are found in the Bible, and He put them there just for you, just like He died just for you. Do not neglect His Word. You will be the reason for a life found lacking, not Him. If you are in tune with Him and walking in the light as He is in the light, you will have fellowship with Him, and nothing will be impossible for you. You will be able to handle anything that life has to throw your way no matter how tough it may be because you'll realize that He is in control and always has been. As the old hymn says, "I surrender all." When we can get to this place, when we surrender all, then it will become easier and easier to embrace His Word for what it is. It is always true and mistake free. What good would it be if it were not?

As Christians we need to let the Holy Spirit lead us, if we battle God we battle our own Spirit, how smart is that? Do not fight God, it is a losing battle. Do however, your own research free from anything but a tall glass of water, a sunlit day, maybe with a few white clouds blowing in the wind, next to the biggest tree around. If you can, find a spot next to the largest body of water near you (an ocean or lake is best but a pool will do) and make sure you have your Bible with you and perhaps a level. Pray under that tree, ponder under that tree, hold your level up and line it up with the body of water in front of you, think under that tree and clear your mind of everything except Gods creation as you watch the sun go down and watch the night sky and the moon and stars take over. Let God's Holy Word permeate your soul and mind there. He wants to give you your heart's desire. Once we are done fantasizing about what our hearts desire is, we will inevitably come to the conclusion that what we really want is the truth.

There is truth in nature. Nature is God's gift to us. If someone wants to debate the real science of creation then they should spend time outside and get away from the chalk board. Look intently at all the incredible things there are out there, the animal life, the sea life, the plants and trees. We cannot make these, only God can make these. Life exists in all these things because God is that life, He imposed His Spirit, His life into all these things and especially into us. I don't intend to ever impose an arrogant attitude in my thoughts and ideas, but I have done these things and it is therapeutic, just good for the soul, like an hour of intense yoga is good for your body. Let God talk to you and you talk to God but be sure to listen. He says in His Word to *"be still and know that I am God" (Psalm 46:10)*. And do this by yourself, just you and God. If you are still not convinced, then sit under that tree and find the verses that support a still sun and a spinning earth.

*John 3:16*, the Christian motto, the truth of the entire Bible wrapped up in one verse—even non-Christians can quote this verse.

> *"For God so loved the world that He gave His only son, that whoever will believe in Him will not perish but have everlasting life" (John 3:16).*

The Gospel, the good news, is a happy ending for those who love their Father and want to spend eternity in heaven being everything that we were supposed to be. Peace, joy, rest, love, and happiness for all time. No more pain, no hurt, no sorrow, no regret. The other option is scary—all the pain, all the hurt, suffering, torment, and regret for all time. Your Father wants the good and happy ending for you. What father wouldn't? You will accept Him or you will reject Him, it's up to you to make that choice. He loves you but won't force you; however, come the end of days the Word says *"that at the name of Jesus every knee will bow, of those who are in heaven and those on the earth, and those under the earth" (Philippians 2:10)*. You can do it freely or you can be forced, but you will bow, and you will confess. Why? Because the Bible says so. The Bible says a lot and it has never been proven wrong. If the Bible has never been proven wrong then… wait for it…the sun moves.

Regarding eternal life and heaven and hell, His choice is clear, and He is giving it away. All you have to do is accept it and say thank you. Fairly easy. Why does every Christian believe this? Because it's in the Bible, and the Bible is true. It is our hope, it is our salvation. Every word was put in the Bible in its special place. We can dissect it, debate it, and reason over it but it is always true in everything it says. How many men and women have set out to prove that the Bible has errors? More often than not these people end up becoming hard core believers because the Word of God got to their very spirit. The Holy Spirit touched them through the Word of God and that is just what happens. The Word of God never comes back void. It's magical, more precisely it's spiritual.

The spiritual world is all around us, good and bad. While aliens and space are not real, angels and demons most assuredly are. Why? Because the Bible says so. Another spoiler alert: the good side wins, but the dark side takes many souls to hell—souls that make the Lord weep. He does not want to lose one sheep, but unfortunately countless men and women will reject His love and His free gift of heavenly bliss for all time. How stupid, how tragic. The devil and his minions know the truth, but they made their choice and have been trying to drag as many of us to hell with them because of their hatred of God since the beginning. The devil schemes his wicked ways 24/7/365, walking back and forth over the earth seeking whom he may devour. He has blinded the masses with fake knowledge intended to confuse, obfuscate, and deny God's truths. Let us not let him win. Pray to the Father for wisdom and let the Holy Spirit move in our lives, oh that we could just get out of the way.

*Isaiah 40:8 says, "The word of God stands forever."*

We can be sure that God made no mistakes in His Word, and it is not going anywhere.

Staying in *Isaiah 40 verses 21 and 22:*

> *Have you not understood from the foundations of the earth? It is He who sits above the circle of the earth, its inhabitants are like grasshoppers. Who stretches out the heavens like a curtain, and spreads them out like a tent to dwell in?*

> *The Creator of the ends of the earth. (Isaiah 40:28)*

> *The ends of the earth were afraid. (Isaiah 41:5)*

> *You whom I have taken from the ends of the earth. (v.9)*

> *From the rising of the sun he shall call My name. (v.25)*

> *Who spread forth the earth. (Isaiah 42:5)*

> *His praise from the ends of the earth. (v.10)*

> *And bring my daughters from the ends of the earth. (Isaiah 43:6)*

> *I am the Lord, who makes all things, who stretches out the heavens all alone, who spreads abroad the earth myself. (Isaiah 44:24)*

> *He makes their knowledge foolishness. (v.25)*

*They may know from the rising of the sun to its setting. (Isaiah 45:6)*

*I have made the earth, and created man on it. I, My hands, stretched out the heavens. (v.12)*

*Who formed the earth and made it, who has established it, who did not create it in vain, who formed it to be inhabited. (v.18)*

*Look to Me and be saved all you ends of the earth. (v.22)*

*Your wisdom and your knowledge have warped you. (Isaiah 47:10)*

*Indeed My hand has laid the foundation of the earth, and My right hand stretched out the heavens. (Isaiah 48:13)*

*Utter it to the ends of the earth. (v.20)*

*That You should be My salvation to the ends of the earth. (Isaiah 49:6)*

*Do not fear the reproach of men, nor be afraid of their insults. (Isaiah 51:7)*

*You forget the Lord your Maker, who stretched out the heavens and laid the foundations of the world. (v.13)*

*I have laid the foundations of the earth. (v.16)*

*All the ends of the earth shall see the salvation of our God. (Isaiah 52:10)*

*They shall fear the name of the Lord and His glory from the rising of the sun. (Isaiah 59:19)*

*Your sun shall no longer go down. (Isaiah 60:20)*

*Indeed the Lord has proclaimed to the end of the world. (Isaiah 62:11)*

There is an end to our world, God Himself made it. The sun rises and the sun sets, the Lord God has said as much. He has given the earth foundations. This quick run through of Isaiah 40 through Isaiah 62 tells us over and over again just how the Lord God did things. If Moses was wrong, then we must assume that Isaiah is also wrong.

Are they wrong?

Each of us gets but one life. Yesterday, I received the news that a brother in the Lord had passed away. I got the text from a friend at my old church that this gentleman had moved on into glory. This brother was an older man, old enough to have been my father. His wife had also passed away a year before him. They were both die-hard Dodger fans who had held season tickets since the Dodgers moved from Brooklyn to Los Angeles back in the late '50s. I was fortunate enough to enjoy those seats on several occasions. They were great seats. But that was not their legacy. Their legacy was much more—it was that of being born-again Christians who always had a smile and plenty of time for those in need. Together they raised a wonderful family and had many grandkids and great grandkids. They were both surrounded by love as they moved into the next life of eternal love. What will be your legacy? How will you be remembered?

I understand that choosing sides on this particular issue will not help your legacy in the eyes of the world. But whose eyes do we want to please? We are told in the Bible that the world will hate us. Do you feel hated? If not, then maybe we are doing something wrong. Wait, what? That's right, we should be hated by the world outside of our Christian brotherhood.

Why? Well, because the Bible said so. God Himself said so. Therefore, if we are not hated, then we must be doing something wrong. Flat earth and a moving sun are offensive issues, so is the cross and both issues will get you hated.

> *"Blessed are you when men hate you, and when they*
> *exclude you, and revile you and cast out your name*
> *as evil, for the Son of man's sake" (Luke 6:22).*

The world has so ostracized the term *flat-earther* that it is synonymous with stupidity. You are considered ignorant if this is your belief. That is some darn good programming. With all the Bible verses shown here and all the practical scientific proofs and experiments, just who are the stupid ones? Just try having a sincere conversation about this with anyone you know and watch the derision and ridicule pour out. Like we've already discussed, most people are so programmed that you're bound to end up in a heated argument if you hold your stance and especially if you offer proof. For every proof you give them, they will attack all the more, never satisfied, always demanding more and more, and when you give them more, the worse it will get. It will end friendships and cause division in our families and in our churches, if we were to become passionate about it. But we should be passionate about it. Truth is truth.

As a house or a building implies that construction workers got together to build, so does creation. God built this place, and He built it according to His blueprints, not man's. It's all been spelled out here for us in His verses, the work has been done for you, but do your own work. Read the Bible for starters. Take your level with you on your next flight. Consider the water in your glass and toilet and pool or in a lake or an ocean.

Consider the rainbow, ponder level buildings, look through the moon on a beautiful clear day, and trust your senses. Be an openminded thinker. "Openminded thinker" has kind of a negative reaction in the church; it congers up the notion of "Hey, man, I'm an open minded thinker. Free love and do what you want and everything is okay if that's how you feel." I disagree. Being openminded to me means that God has given me a well-functioning brain, that I am free to use it to the best of my abilities, and that I should not accept information as fact just because everybody else does. Being a Christian for as long as I have been has been an amazing journey. One of the truths that was learned along the way is this: trust your senses, as born-again believers our senses are the Holy Spirit guiding us, our senses are from God Himself. He alone gave us our DNA, our emotions, and every other attribute we have.

As Christians we are ridiculed for believing in all the biblical miracles and for believing that there even is a God and that He loves us and that He died for our sins and, even still, He rose from the dead and He promised that if we believe in Him that He will come again and take us to heaven where we will never die and never have pain or sorrow. We are all already considered stupid. Do not be fooled; the world already hates us. So if we are already hated, then let us stand for the obvious truth of God's Word and let us also stand against the obvious lie that our world moves and that our sun does not. Don't look behind the curtain, kid, or it will be made crystal clear to you. All the globes in the classrooms across the world are tools to program us at the most critical time in our lives. It's only true because it's all we've ever known. It is and has been "the greatest lie on earth." What are your senses telling you? Listen to the Spirit.

The world has been programmed so successfully that this seems to be a near impossible task to overcome, but that does not mean that we don't try. It is a noble cause; it is the truth of God Himself. It cannot be made more clear. It can be understood that the non-Christian would have more trouble conquering the programming, but the born-again Christian has the Word of God to help them overcome and the Spirit of God Himself inside of us to help us discern truth from lies. We just have to read His Holy Word, it's all right there in plain sight. We truly will be stupid if we don't take advantage of reading the most important book of all time, written by God Himself.

# CHAPTER 14

# Infiltrated

*But though we, or an angel from heaven, preach
any other gospel unto you than that which we have
preached unto you, let him be accursed.*

*—Galatians 1:8*

We rely on our resources. The Bible was the main resource for this book. I knew that my own opinions and thoughts would be scrutinized, so a lot of research and reading went into making sure that what was being written down was as accurate, as I am passionate. A ton of reading and cross-referencing other books has helped tremendously and only reinforced the beliefs shared here. It helps to also be able to bounce ideas off of other humans. As my wife and son would get tired at times debating me, I enlisted some friends without letting on that a book was being created.

These are mature Christian older adults that are successful in the world as well as being amazing friends. They listened and asked questions and then started studying some of this topic on their own. They agree that the points laid out are compelling, yet they still have that programming to overcome. Even with scientific proof and biblical truth that indeed match up nicely with each other, my friends come short of being able to say with the confidence that I have that the sun moves. However, just recently one of these friends did confess to me that he no longer believes that we went to the moon. Smart man, and he grew up loving all things space. His realization crushed him. Who doesn't love Star Trek and Captain Kirk?

Other books have been referenced in this book—some good and some not so good and some so off course that they must have been written deliberately as to try and align today's "common knowledge" with the Bible. They fall woefully short. You could say that they have been weighed in the balance and have been found lacking. One such book was under my own roof. My wife has a women's study Bible that tries, with no biblical proof or any other proof, to describe the verses in Joshua concerning the sun stopping.

I quote from that Bible in its commentary side notes: "*Perhaps* the earth tilted so that Israel would experience a northern-type long day, *or* the *rotation* of the earth *may have* slowed." This found in a "Nelsons" New King James Women's Study Bible.

Did you catch that?

Perhaps? Or? Rotation? May have? The earth slowed or the earth tilted?

How about what the Bible said? The sun stood still.

We don't need conjecture and speculation, and we don't need maybes because someone wants the Bible to conform to the world's view. This is blatant and obvious deception being hung around our necks. And now you not only have to be aware that you get a New King James Bible, but you have to make sure you check to see who the publisher is so that you can get your new Bible without the psychobabble and space talk in it.

It is this kind of commentary that makes it unnecessary for Satan to even bother with trying to change the words of the Bible or removing them, we are doing it for him. While this person's commentary is not in the Bible, it is in the Bible, right next to the scriptures, sharing pages and thus can be very confusing as to give this conjecture more credence by placing it side by side next to the actual scriptures.

Another one of my friends loaned me their copy of *Nelsons Illustrated Bible Dictionary*, and while I have refrained mentioning some of the titles and authors of other books that I used as resources, I have no problem mentioning this book.

On page 332 and page 333 of the 1986/1995 revised edition, my friend found this and shared it with me. Looking up the phrase "earth, four corners of the," it says, "People of Bible times thought that the earth was flat, they knew nothing of a spherical earth which orbited the sun!"

While this book has many helpful descriptions of words used in Bible days, it has been corrupted. The authors obviously knew nothing about what they wrote. They just went blindly along with what the world believes. Zero facts. Zero proof. Or they did know and it was done on purpose—which must be the case, and that is scary. Contradictions committed on purpose to mislead the masses and now to mislead the Christian church, straight from Satan himself.

This book undermines itself on the next page. Looking up "Earth, pillars of," it says the idea that the earth is supported by pillars or upon a foundation of some sort is found often in the Old Testament. Also, that they thought the heavens were a solid dome above the earth.

Under "earth, vaulted"—they correctly state that the word *vault* actually means "something held firmly together," and again "founded His strata in the earth." Under the heading "Earth, the newer", we see the word *universe* being used again.

For once and for all, there is no such thing as a universe. It is a made-up word! We live under a hard-protected sky. He placed the earth and the heavens and the sun and the moon and the stars in it. Period! When we cannot trust our own resources and Bibles and supposed educated Christian men and women of God to get it right, what chance does anyone have of finding out the truth?

I let you in on what happened at my home Bible study a few weeks back. Well, it happened again. Same study three weeks later and the same pastor teaching.

Once again, I agreed with this pastor for 99 percent of his message, however, he once again used an analogy using "gravity" as a main point and repeatedly used the word *universe*. Again, same result; no one spoke up, no one objected. It's the same issue with these books and commentaries, we read the babble in them and then no one speaks up. They are allowed to stand. Back to our *Illustrated Bible Dictionary*, on page 1093 the book outs its own contradiction. *Nelsons Bible Dictionary* describes the sun as the heavenly body that rises in the morning (moves). On the same page; "He interrupted the suns' regular course". "The sun stood still" for Joshua, and it "went backwards" for Hezekiah. (Joshua 10:13; Isaiah 38:8). If it went backwards, then it had to have been moving forward! Wait, back on page 332, this same book stated that the earth orbits a non-moving sun.

Can we trust nothing? Are we "woke"? Does anyone care that we are being forced to worship the sun and anything else besides the one true God who gave us this incredible place to live? Also, on page 332 of this book, it describes Earth as the "planet" on which we live. It's not a *planet*, that is made up word that means nothing.

The internet can and is sometimes used for good, much of the research for this book was done by looking up many resources that years ago would have required dozens of trips to the library.

A site called hebrew4christians.com, for example. It was easy to search the word *earth* on this site. Immediately the site provides a fake round earth picture and says in its very first sentence, "Looking at earth from space, it is evident that the planet is covered with water." According to NASA, water covers. Blah, blah, blah, you lost me with (space and planet and NASA).

Once again, a little truth like the fact that we have a lot of water on earth mixed with words like *planet* and *space*. Again, zero proof, just accept these terms without question. Sorry, not sorry. We are questioning—moreover, we are providing proof. Where is the world's proof? Shouldn't the world have to defend the globe? Why is the burden of proof placed on those of us who believe in a moving sun? We probably should just slink away with our tails between our legs, but wait, we have the Word of God! And God's laws are backed up by science. His laws don't change. Water will always seek to be level because that's the way that God set it up. He could have made water curve on a round spinning planet, but He didn't.

We have been infiltrated.

Here is some more paranoia for you, as already shown: we can't trust a lot of literature that's been written since the New King James Bible was introduced. Far as I can tell, the New King James version of God's Holy Word has not been compromised depending on the publisher. But other newer versions definitely have been. When you take words out of the Bible and replace them with other words, that is exactly what you have done. The word *worlds* was replaced with *universe*, the word *circle* was replaced with the word *sphere*—we could make another long list of Bible verses that have been changed or manipulated here for you, but you get the idea. The words that indicate the shape of our world have been changed in our newer Bibles.

Should we wonder why?

Replacing the word *worlds* with *universe* changes the entire meaning of the verse, as does replacing the word *circle* with the word *sphere*. A sphere indicates a ball, a three dimensional object, where as a circle is a circle, a shape, just like a square or a triangle, not three dimensional. The world is not a triangle, just like it is not a ball. Our hebrew4christians website also provided this for describing when looking up the word *sun*. Its description was this: "The daily rising sun was a symbol of creation."

Well, they got that one right, didn't they? The sun indeed rises and moves about under our sky. Contradictions everywhere. My very own New King James Bible that I mentioned earlier has a picture of a globe in it on one of the maps in the back of the Bible. It's just there—no reason and no explanation given, just more reinforcement.

*"Do not be carried about with various and strange doctrines"* (Hebrews 13:9).

This notion that we move and the sun does not is indeed a strange doctrine, it is pagan. It is sun worship, it is wrong, and it is sin. So far, we have listed almost a hundred Bible verses in support of a moving sun and a nonmoving earth. What verses does the church have in support of an earth spinning like a basketball on a Globetrotters' finger? What pastor can dance around this? What verses will he use?

There are none. The Christian church, its pastors, leaders, and members have become complicit in the perpetuation of the lie. The

Bible dictionary that my friend loaned me has the word *suicide* in it. Why is this important? It is important because the definition is as follows:

*Suicide.* "The act of taking one's own life. The word *suicide* does not occur in the Bible." Wait, stop! It goes on, but it has said enough.

The fact that this Bible dictionary included a word that they said is not in the Bible is enough. As we saw earlier the words "planet" and "universe" are not in the Bible either, neither does this dictionary have any definition for them.

However, this dictionary has no problem in using these words: *planet, universe, Venus,* and a lot more to describe other words that it does list.

The closest word to universe listed in this Bible dictionary is *unicorn* on page 1164. Other words not listed in this Bible dictionary and rightly so are Neptune, Saturn, Mars, Pluto, Uranus, Jupiter, Venus, and Mercury. God placed the sun and the moon and the stars in the firmament. He knows the stars by name.

He named the earth and the sun and the moon and the stars. He did not name "planets" because there are no planets. Go back a few chapters and look at the list of names again that we humans gave these "planets". Notice the pure paganism. God's Word says He named the stars and a few of them are mentioned in Amos 5:8, Pleiades and Orion. Do we think He would have named planets after other satanic Greek gods if He did make them? And why are all the pictures round balls? Science and observation tell us that nothing in nature is the same yet we accept that all other "planets" are basically the same round balls. This defies science. The debate process on this issue continues to make the case for God's Word.

My son has a good mind, and as we own a business together, we can spend a lot of time on the road together. This is great quality time that we sometimes spend talking and debating this and many other issues. He observed the other day that he looks at things a lot differently now, knowing the truth about our world. When you look up at the sky and see the wondrous blue above and know that a loving God is protecting us from the waters above and that He promised that He would never again open those doors to flood our world, it is comforting. To know that we are immoveable and not spinning out of control, flying through space at thousands of miles per hour is reassuring.

In short, knowing that God has created a wonderful, beautiful, and safe home for us is what you would expect a loving Father to provide for His children. You would also expect Him to not make it complicated to understand. He wants us to know about it. That's what all the Bible verses are about. It is overwhelming once you let go of what you have been programmed to think is true. Only God is true. Let every man be a liar, and we are. We lie to ourselves and to others so that we are not singled out as a conspiracy nut or stupid, crazy, misguided, or possessed. Jesus was accused of having the power of demons—demons!

It's in the Bible—the so-called smart people of His day accused the Creator of having the power to heal as coming from Satan! The so-called intellects of today will deride and dismiss us and our Bible because of this one issue. This is where the rubber meets the road. Will we defend the Word of God? Will we defend God? Or is this just a big joke? I don't think that God is laughing about this. His word unequivocally sates that the sun moves and the earth does not. Is the Bible wrong? The fact that the sun moves and it is described as moving throughout the entire Bible in almost every book of the Bible is so overwhelming that one sermon will not do. One little clever way of interpreting a passage or two will just not do.

This message should be preached every Sunday in every pulpit for years to come to undo what has been done to our faith, to our beliefs, to our culture, to our parents, grandparents, children, and grandchildren, to the truth, to our Bible and our God.

> "A lie can travel around the world and back again while the truth is lacing up its boots" (Mark Twain).

If something is true, you don't have to keep trying to reinforce it with propaganda, but that is what we get. Day after day, year after year, we have the false image of a round, spinning earth floating in space shoved down our throats. It started way back before radio, before movies, before TV, and since the invention of all these mediums each one has been used to indoctrinate us into the cult of sun worship. That's what that huge list of "space movies" was about. If you believe that the sun is stationary and that the earth moves, you are part of a cult belief system.

Hollywood? Infiltrated.

Media? Infiltrated.

Politics and government? Infiltrated.

Books and radio? Infiltrated.

Christian doctrine? Infiltrated.

Pulpits? I'd argue, infiltrated.

If one part of the Bible is wrong, then maybe the whole thing could be wrong, or do we get to pick and choose what to believe? How about all those crazy miracles? Which ones do we get to choose to believe in? I believe that dead people will live again, or I believe that an ocean was parted, and millions of people walked through it on dry land. I believe that the Bible states the sun moves and the earth does not. Which is harder to accept? The Bible has all the answers about this and much more in its pages. The Bible is alive. It is the living word of God himself. It does not lie, it does not confuse, it does not have contradictions, it is not wrong, it is the most real truth that we have ever had about anything—period. And we better embrace it and hold on tight because they will be coming for our Bibles soon.

This topic of our world is actually nothing new. There are two books in my library that were written in the eighteen hundreds— *Zetetic Astronomy (Earth Is Not a Globe)* by Samuel Birley Rowbotham (1849), and *One Hundred Proofs That the Earth Is Not a Globe* by WM Carpenter (1885). Both are fascinating reads. I mentioned these books earlier, and if you want all the experiments and math and science behind a moving sun and a still earth, I refer you to these two books along with the also mentioned book titled *The Greatest Lie on Earth* by Edward Hendrie (2016), a more updated and easy to read account of all the fake news that's being pushed on us not just daily but moment by moment in almost every book, movie, and TV show.

I bring them up again to make this point: where are the books titled "One hundred proofs that the world *is* a round spinning globe"? Like the sermons that were never preached, we don't need books like that because everybody just knows beyond any shadow of doubt that the earth is a round, spinning globe. Period.

We don't need to discuss it. It is just proven fact. We went to the moon, we came from monkeys, we have planets, and we have NASA and our governments to verify and to believe in and trust. Think about this: someone made it possible to name the craters of the moon after individuals or they paid their way onto the list, I'm not sure. There are some recognizable names on this list, and the sheer number of names is impressive, but why would so many people want to be on this list? The earth is far more important and much bigger—makes you wonder. Here's a not so quick part of the list.

| Ernst Abbe | Charles Greeley Abbot | Niels Henrik Abel | Antonio Abetti | Giorgio Abetti | Abu Abdullah al-Bakri |
|---|---|---|---|---|---|
| Abu al-Wafa al-Buzjani | Charles Hitchcock Adams | John Couch Adams | Walter Sydney Adams | Agatharchides | Agrippa |
| Pierre d'Ailly | George Biddell Airy | Roberts Grant Aitken | Ajima Naonobu | Harold Alden | Kurt Alder |
| Buzz Aldrin | Nikolai Alekhin | Alexander the Great | Alfonso X of Castile | Alfraganus | Dinsmore Alter |
| Florentino Ameghino | Giovanni Battista Amici | Ammonius Saccas | Guillaune Amontons | Ronald Amundsen | Anaxagoras |
| Anaximander | Anaximenes of Miletus | Karen Andel | William Anders | John August Anderson | Leif Erland Anderson |
| Aleksandr Andronov | (last names only from here on out, just too many names… ridiculous) | Ango | Anders Jonas Angstrom | Ann | Annegrit |
| Ansgarius | Antoniadi | Anuchin | Anville | Apianus | Apollo |
| Apollonius | Appleton | Arago | Aratus | Archimedes | Archytas |
| Argelander | Ariadaeus | Aristarchus | Aristillus | Aristoteles | Arminski |
| Armstrong | Arnold | Arrhenius | Artamonov | Artem'ev | Artemis |

| Artimovich | Aryabhata | Arzachel | Asada | Asclcepi | Ashbrook |
|---|---|---|---|---|---|
| Aston | Atlas | Atwood | Autolycus | Auwers | Auzout |
| Avicenna | Avogadro | Azophi | Baade | Babakin | Babbage |
| Babcock | Back | Backlund | Baco | Baillaud | Bailly |
| Baily | Balandin | Balboa | Baldet | Ball | Balmer |
| Banachiewicz | Bancroft | Banting | Barbier | Barkla | Barnard |
| Barocius | Barring | Barrow | Bartels | Bawa | Bayer |
| Beals | Beaumont | Becquerel | Becvar | Beer | Behaim |
| Beijerinck | Beketov | Bela | Belkovich | Bell | Bellinsgauzen |
| Ballot | Belopol'skiy | Belyaev | Benedict | Bergman | Bergstrand |
| Berkner | Brerlage | Bernoulli | Berosus | Berzelius | Bessarion |
| Bessel | Bettinus | Bhabha | Bianchini | Biela | Bilharz |
| Billy | Bingham | Biot | Birkeland | Birkhoff | Birmingham |
| Birt | Bi Sheng | Bjerknes | Black | Blackett | Blagg |
| Blancanus | Blanchard | Blanchinus | Blazhko | Bliss | Bobillier |
| Bob one | Bode | Bioethics | Boguslawsky | Bohnenberger | Bohr |
| Bok | Boltzmann | Bolyai | Bombelli | Bondarenko | Bonpland |
| Boole | Borda | Borel | Boris | Borman | Born |
| Borya | Bosch | Boscovich | Bose | Boss | Boggier |
| Boussingault | Bowditch | Bowen | Boyle | Bracket | Bragg |
| Brasher | Brad | Bradley | Bredikhin | Breislak | Brenner |
| Brewster | Brianchon | Bridgman | Briggs | Brisbane | Bronk |
| Brouwer | Brown | Bruce | Brunner | Buch | Buffon |
| Buisson | Bullialdus | Bunsen | Burckhardt | Burg | Burn ham |
| Busting | Butler | Buys-Ballot | Byrd | Byrgius | C. Herschel |
| C. Mayer | Cabanas | Cabers | Cailleux | Cai Lun | Canal |
| Cajori | Ca;ippus | Cameron | Campanus | Campbell | Cannizzaro |
| Cannon | Cantor | Capella | Capuanus | Cardanus | Carlini |
| Carlos | Carmichael | Carnot | Carol | Carpenter | Carrel |
| Carrillo | Harrington | Cartan | Carver | Casts | Cassegrain |
| Cassini | Catalan | Catharina | Cauchy | Cavalerius | Cavendish |
| Caventou | Cayley | Celsius | Censorious | Cepheus | Chacornac |

| | | | | | |
|---|---|---|---|---|---|
| Chadwick | Chaffee | Challis | Chalonge | Chamberlin | Champollion |
| Chandler | Chang Heng | Chang-Ngo | Chant | Chaplygin | Chapman |
| Chappe | Chappell | Charles | Charlier | Chaucer | Chauvenet |
| Chawla | Chebyshev | Chernyshev | Chevallier | Ching-Te | Chladni |
| Chretien | Cichus | Clairaut | Clark | Clausius | Clavius |
| Cleomedes | Cleostratus | Clerke | Coblentz | Cockcroft | Collins |
| Compton | Comrie | Comstock | Condon | Condorcet | Congreve |
| Canon | Cook | Cooper | Copernicus | Cori | Coriolis |
| Couder | Coulomb | Courtney | Cremona | Crile | Crocco |
| Crommelin | Crookes | Crozier | Cruger | Ctesibius | Curie |
| Curtis | Curtius | Cusanus | Cuvier | Cyrano | Cyrillus |
| Cysatus | D. Brown | da Vinci | Daedalus | Dag | Daguerre |
| Dale | d'Alembert | Dalton | Daly | Damoiseau | Daniell |
| Donjon | Dante | Carney | D'Arrest | D'Arsonval | Darwin |
| Das | Daubree | Davisson | Davy | Dawes | Dawson |
| De Forest | de Gasparis | de Gerlache | De La Rue | De Moraes | De Morgan |
| De Roy | De Sitter | De Vico | De Vries | Debes | Debut |
| Debye | Chechen | Delambre | Delaunay | Delia | Delisle |
| Dellinger | Delmonte | Deplore | Deluc | Dembrowski | Democritus |
| Demonax | Denning | Desargues | Descartes | Deseilligny | Deslandres |
| Deutsch | Dewar | Diana | Diderot | Dionysius | Diophantus |
| Dirichelet | Dobrovol'skiy | Doerfel | Dolled | Donati | Donna |
| Donner | Doppelmayer | Doppler | Douglass | Dove | Draper |
| Drebbel | Dreyer | Drude | Dryden | Drygalski | Dubyago |
| Dufay | Dugan | Duner | Dunthorne | Dyson | Dziewulski |
| Eckert | Eddington | Edison | Edith | Egede | Ehrlich |
| Eichstadt | Eijkman | Eimmart | Einstein | Einthoven | Elger |
| Kellerman | Ellison | Elmer | Elvey | Emden | Neck |
| Endymion | Engel'gardt | Eotvos | Epigenes | Epimenides | Eratosthenes |
| Erlanger | Erro | Esclangon | Esnault-Pelterie | Espin | Euclides |
| Euctemon | Exdoxus | Euler | Evans | Evdokimov | Evershed |

| Ewen | Fabbroni | Fabricius | Fairy | Fahrenheit | Fairouz |
| Friday | Faustino | Faith | Faye | Fechner | Fedora |
| Felix | Fenyi | Feoktistov | Fermat | Fermi | Ferneries |
| Ferryman | Fesenkov | Feuillee | Fibiger | Finsch | Finsen |
| Firmicus | First | Fischer | Fitzgerald | Fizeau | Flammarion |
| Flamsteed | Fleming | Florensky | Florey | Focas | Fontana |
| Fontenelle | Foster | Foucault | Fourier | Fowler | Fox |
| Fra Mauro | Fracastorius | Franck | Franklin | Franz | Fraunhofer |
| Fredholm | Freud | Freundlich | … | … | … |

We are not even through the *F*s yet.

This list goes on through the rest of the alphabet but that would be a waste of paper. That's a lot of people that, in my opinion, are engaging in moon worship. What else can it be? Did you see your families name on the list? I, for one, want no part of my family's name being associated with the moon. I want my name listed in the Book of Life, and it is! Praise the Lord!

"We don't need some old, antiquated Bible telling us that science is wrong, that we are wrong. We are humans, we are smart, we are in charge of this world, and if we want to say it's a spinning planet with a rolling moon and an unmoving sun, then who is God to tell us any different?"

When Moses came down from the mountain with the Ten Commandments to find the children (adults) worshiping an image of gold and engaging in all sorts of sexual perversions, it was an excellent example of how we humans act if left to our own devices, and this happened after they saw God open up a sea for them to walk through. Have we learned nothing? We worship a spinning globe!

It might as well be a golden calf.

God did not choose to send His son to earth in our time. He took care of that two thousand-plus years ago. We do not see first-hand miracles being performed today, and even if we did, we would probably forget that we saw an ocean open up for us, and we too would turn to idol worship and sexual perversions. Oh wait, we have already done that, just like the people who actually did walk through the ocean. We have bought into the propaganda and lies hook, line, and sinker. Our churches now preach against what the Bible says about the sun moving and the earth standing still and firm.

However, it will not do to just change a word or two in the Bible anymore because the sheer amount of verses provided in God's Word regarding the sun moving is just too overwhelming. There are just too many of them. God must have done this on purpose because He knew what was coming. Hence, I believe that the Bible will be deemed dangerous and that it will be banned at some point—even in America as it has been banned in other countries. If you adhere to what the Bible says about the earth and sun and will under no circumstances change your mind, you will be labeled ignorant and a danger to normal society. Once labeled, good luck keeping a job or friends. We see the Ten Commandments being taken down in public places. You can't carry a Bible at school. You can't pray at a football game. Sex and nudity are the normal. Homosexuality is in every movie and television show. It is accepted. God does not accept it.

The utter chaos that this issue alone will cause throughout the world will be enough reason for the world's governments to outlaw our Bible and those who believe in it. Are we okay with our Christianity as it is? Believing in some but not all of the Bible. Which stories are true, and which are false? This is blockbuster stuff.

You would think that reading the Bible as much as I did in writing this book would be considered a good thing, that all the cross referencing and fact checks and Hebrew and Greek definitions would be considered good Bible study. This will not be the case. As a matter of fact, if you are reading this, it will be a small miracle that this book was ever published. But there is no doubt when it is published and sold, the Christian community will resist it, deny its validity, and recommend that believers should not read it, and that fact should speak volumes. Truth is truth and cannot be hidden forever.

I asked you previously to do you own poll, to take your own survey. I did. I did it with friends and family. That didn't turn out well. I did it with strangers, and it also did not turn out well. I did it with Christians and nonbelievers. The reaction is always the same—ridicule, laughter, and scorn. This coming from believers in God, in

Jesus, in the Bible. It proves the point that cognitive dissonance is real. We are past the point of no return however and I am no longer concerned about a reputation with men. I will never be able to make the world my friend. The world is my enemy, and God is my friend. He is also the author of the Bible that reinforces and is in fact is the sole and only needed source for information about our world. He did make it after all, and He didn't forget how He did it. As a matter of fact, He wrote it all down so we could all know and appreciate and not forget.

I quote from *The Greatest Lie on Earth* page 340:

> Modern science has replaced God's abode of heaven with the myth of the empty vacuum of space, thus suggesting that there is no heaven and there is no God. If there is only an empty vacuum of space, that means that God cannot be above us walking in the circuit of heaven. *"Thick clouds are a covering to Him, that He sees not; and He walks in the circuit of heaven"* (Job 22:14).

Our *Nelsons Illustrated Bible Dictionary* undoes itself again while trying to explain the four corners of the earth as mentioned in Isaiah 11: 12 and in many other passages as well by explaining that it should be expressed today as "from every point of the compass." Excuse me? Did the writer of this nonsense not realize what they were saying? A compass is a perfect example of how our system works—a flat circle. He drew a circle in the deep. He gave us limits as to how far we can go. He set up boundaries with walls of ice to keep our waves back. Another definition for the word *compass* is "a circular boundary." We don't fall off of a flat earth because God designed it perfectly to contain everything in it including us. There are indeed corners as well that we can't see, but they are there because the Bible tells us so. Believe it or not, the Bible does require us humans to have a little faith, even if it is only the size of a mustard seed.

The verbiage *face of* is strewn throughout the pages of the Bible. There is a face of a compass, there is a face on your head, there is a face of our world. The back of the head is not used as a description of our world. There is a face to a clock—there is no face to a baseball or basketball or a globe.

God moved upon the *face of* the waters. (Genesis 1:2)

I have given you every herb bearing seed upon the *face of* all the earth. (Genesis 1:29)

A mist from the earth watered the whole *face of* the ground. (Genesis 2:6)

Thou have driven me out this day from the *face of* the earth. (Genesis 4:14)

When men began to multiply on the *face of* the earth. (Genesis 6:1)

I will destroy man whom I have created from the *face of* the earth. (Genesis 6:7)

To keep the seed alive upon the *face of* the earth. (Genesis 7:3)

I will destroy from off the *face of* the earth. (Genesis 7:4)

And the ark went upon the *face of* the waters. (Genesis 7:18)

And every living thing was destroyed which was upon the *face of* the earth. (Genesis 7:23)

He sent forth a dove to see it the waters were abated from off the *face of* the ground. (Genesis 8:8)

And she returned unto him into the ark, for the waters were on the *face of* the whole earth. (Genesis 8:9)

And behold the *face of* the ground was dry. (Genesis 8:13)

Let us make a name lest we be scattered abroad upon the *face of* the whole earth. (Genesis 11:4)

So the Lord scattered them abroad from there upon the *face of* all the earth. (Genesis 11:8)

The Lord did there confound the language of all the earth and from there the Lord did scatter them abroad upon the *face of* all the earth. (Genesis 11:9)

The famine was over all the *face of* the earth. (Genesis 41:56)

And he bowed himself with his *face to* the earth. (Genesis 48:12)

And they shall cover the *face of* the earth. (Exodus 10:5)

Okay, that's a lot of verses about the face of the earth, and we only got through Genesis. I added one verse in Exodus to show that this continues throughout the Bible. If you want more verses, just type in the word *face* in your Bible app and enjoy all the verses for yourself.

There is indeed a face to our earth, and we are like the circle of a compass. A globe ball earth does not have a face. Can a spinning ball be flooded? where would all the water go into the channels that God said He made for the overflowing of water? It would be much easier to flood a stationary plane. Things clearly do not add up in support of a globe earth; things clearly do add up for what the Bible says we do live in.

This worldwide vast conspiracy is in everything and everywhere. Did you know that the Harper Collins publishing company is responsible for the publishing of Anton LaVey's *Satanic Bible* and *The Joy of Gay Sex*?

The same Harper Collins company is also the publisher of the *Nelsons Illustrated Bible Dictionary* that I am currently borrowing from my friend and have been using for reference, as well as the already mentioned *Womens Study Bible* belonging to my wife. Maybe it's not so shocking; the interwoven mess that Satan has strung together through our companies and movies and television and science and entertainment and culture and sex and sports and even our churches and Bibles is enough for another book.

One last mention of Mr. Hendrie's book. After all, I do have my own book to finish. In his section detailing the corruption that has taken place in our own Bibles, he says on page 352 that "the NIV version of the Bible is the most popular of the new Bible versions, and that the NIV represents 45% of all Bibles sold today. Dr. Virginia Mollenkott, the textual style editor for the NIV, is an admitted lesbian. The chairman of the NIV Old Testament committee, Dr. Woudstra, was considered to be sympathetic to the interests and practices of sodomites. The NIV chief editor vaunted the fact that the NIV showed that it is a great error to believe that in order to be born-again, one has to have faith in Jesus as Savior." Heresy!

Do you own a copy of the NIV Bible? we do.

I, however, have been using only the New King James Bible for years in my own personal study and will now only grab another version to compare them with the older, more correct versions. Do not be misled. Satan is smarter than you and me. He has been around a long time and will not let go of his victories easily. He has managed to make cracks in our own Bibles and study materials. He sees the round earth as a victory—done and won. That much is certain. It begs the question: should we be using these reference books if errors have been found in them by a novice. I think that the answer is yes, if only to prove the point of everything being corrupted. Please do take the time to invest and read these other books mentioned here. They are sound and have no conflict with the Word of God. This book you are now reading is about what the Word of God says concerning our creation and is directed to born again Christians and their leaders and pastors. This book is pleading with our pastors and leaders to please reexamine what you think you know compared to what the Bible clearly says. Get off the fence, quit dancing around it, and quit ignoring it. We owe the church and our members the truth. God Himself requires it of us. If you teach from the Word of God, then teach everything from the Word of God.

> *Solid food belongs to those who are of full age, that is, those who by reason of use have their senses exercised to discern both good and evil. (Hebrews 5:14)*

> *My brethren, let not many of you become teachers, knowing that we shall receive a stricter judgment. (James 3:1)*

Pastors, please let your tongue be tame when defending Satan's ploys regarding our habitation, and let it be on fire when preaching the whole and true word of God and His amazing creation.

> *"Man does not live by bread alone, but by every word that proceeds from the mouth of God" (Luke 4:4).*

So you're labeled the "church of the flat earth"? So what! Truth is truth. How can we ask the church body to keep swallowing a lie?

How long will this go on? What is our roll in all of this? Like the movie *The Matrix*, once you take the pill, it's all over. The scales will fall from your eyes and you too will be free—free to declare that indeed, every word from God in His Bible is true. The sun moves, and the earth stands still forever. Our role is to proclaim God to a lost world and to know what it is that we believe in.

"Thank you, Lord, for this amazing and awesome gift. Please help the unbeliever become a believer. Please help Christians discover the true and wonderful world that You made for us to live in. Lord, please bring our pastors and leaders to an undeniable understanding that the world has mislead us for far too long and give them the faith and courage that they will need to stand in the face of ridicule and hate coming their way if they have ears to hear.

Father let your words, not mine, convince them. Let you and you alone be glorified. Help us sinners to understand and give us a peace that we can't understand. Guide our every step and prove to this world that you do not lie, you do not confuse. You are the one and only true and righteous God, Creator of all things." Amen.

> *Blessed are those who are persecuted for righteousness sake, for theirs is the kingdom of heaven. Blessed are you when they revile and persecute you, and say all kinds of evil against you falsely for my sake. Rejoice and be exceedingly glad, for great is your reward in heaven, for so they persecuted the prophets who were before you. (Matthew 5:10–11)*

Will we who believe that the Bible is true when it tells us that the earth does not move but the sun does be persecuted? You tell me. How do you feel about all this? All these Bible verses, were they used to support a position? Pastors, are you mad? Being called out is not fun, especially when you are wrong, and you know it. I did not use any of these verses out of context, at least not on purpose. I have prayed much over this issue, I have dug into the Bible and many other resources to write this book. Could I have missed something?

Did I miss something? I most sincerely searched for evidence to tell me otherwise and found none.

Absolutely every verse found in the Bible led to other verses in support of these findings. Not once was anything found in the Bible in support of the globe model of our world. Moreover, we found that the lie of a moving earth has permeated newer Bibles and study material and our official Bible dictionary and other books specifically written about Genesis and other books of the Bible. We don't need to just fight the world on this. Rather, we need to win the fight within our own faith first. We need to become a united church on this and call it what it is. This is war, and it will be the biggest challenge that the church has ever faced. It will cause heated arguments and hopefully prayerful and intense, instructive debate. The fact that good Christian men and women will get so upset at this is just more proof that we have all been successfully programmed. What other issue does the world and the church agree on like this one? Both the world and the church agree that the earth orbits around the unmoving sun, but that's not what the Bible says. We the church have rolled over and played dead, and it's time to come alive and take the fight back because the Bible is right. Take a leap of faith and decide for yourself. Study your own Bible and earnestly pray for clarity about what you read.

Pastors, it's up to you. You have been given the challenge and it is a challenge directly from God's words, not mine. Can any pastor who knows and studies the Word come up with a different conclusion other than the Bible is correct? I think not, and I hope not. The dance with the world is over. It's time to dance with the one who brought you to this party. Let every man be a liar and let God be true.

What is hoped for is to finally have the church address the huge elephant in the room concerning our faith and our belief in our Bible and that we discontinue the lies and infiltration of the devil in our teachings of God's Word!

Pastors need to be called out first, as they are the ordained ones who have been given their authority by God to preach His Word and teach and instruct us. I absolutely love my pastors at my church, but they are wrong on this issue and need to be called out. If the pastors and leaders of our churches won't touch this, then the congregation of the church must. If it comes down to us demanding our leaders to engage, then that is what we must do. Where is that one sermon? Where is the yearlong study about it? Where are the books and movies? Take this book to them. Make them answer.

The peace and comfort that the truth brings is sweet. It may be hell to deal with in the world and even in our own churches, but the verse "*The truth shall set you free*" is applicable in many areas, and this is surely one of them. Once you know, you know. You will now be held accountable for what you know or for what you deny. It's your choice, just like salvation is your choice. The question has been asked repeatedly throughout this book.

What are you going to do about it?

If you decide to embrace God's whole word and His whole truth please beware, it will not be easy. You will be called everything under the moving sun. Life will not be easy for you from now on, but life is a war for the Christian already. It always has been.

# CHAPTER 15

## Mankind

*All things were made by him; and without him was not anything made that was made.*

—*John 1:3*

God is eternal. God's Word is eternal. Our souls are eternal. Earth and heaven are eternal. This world as we know it will not always be the way it is now however; all things will be made new. Mankind likes new, the advertisers know this and market the "new and improved" latest cool gadget or car. Our quiver is indeed full of incredible advances in the material world, the medical world, the world of science, entertainment, and the world of comfort. Yet we have made all these advances using materials placed here by God, and we show no signs of appreciation to Him, only haughty pride in our own accomplishments. Mankind has indeed shown just how incredibly smart we are, as well as how arrogant we are. What incredible machines that we hold in the palm of our hands. But we are addicted to them and in a way worship them. We are to worship God and God alone (*Exodus 20:3*). We have incredible luxuries that we take for granted. The generation of today has no idea of life without even a microwave.

We were one of the first families on our block to get one, somewhere around the mid to late 1970s, not too long ago. King Solomon was the richest man who ever lived, and he never had a microwave oven or got to sleep on memory foam mattresses like we do. Pretty sure he didn't have indoor plumbing either. We have that as well. He never ate the best foods in the world—tacos and pizza, frozen or take out. Remember, the fastest thing on earth used to be a horse. Now we can have breakfast in New York and lunch in Los Angeles on the same day. We have forgotten where we came from.

Every life comes from God. All life, of every kind, comes from God! He made all of this for us, and we deny Him His glory by spouting lies about fictional words like *gravity* and *space curve* and *earth wobble*, etc. And we go along with changing words in the Bible. The NIV is put together by a multi-group committee of all various religions coming together to create this version of the Bible. In the rules, it is stated that words in the Holy Bible are only changed if 70 percent of these committee members agree. What? You only had 30 percent that didn't agree on words like *circle* being changed to *sphere* and *worlds* being changed to *universe*. So very sad that this has happened to well-intentioned men and women who just went along with the ones who are not so well-intentioned. Does it matter if you get 100 percent consensus? you don't change the Word of God period! This is what happens when man gets too full of himself. This has always been a war, and it's been going on a long time. We dismiss God, we have lost our connection with Him, and He will not try forever. We must engage in the fight, consequences be dammed, because He is coming back, and when He does, we want to be found as having fought the good fight. At some point in time, all will be made right, and wicked sinners like us will have to answer for leading others to believe in the lies of Satan about many things, including changing His holy words and buying into the worlds false theory's and speculations. Because that's what it is—pure speculation. Man can't be right about the sun not moving because that makes God wrong about the sun moving.

It seems that we are too comfortable today; life is too easy. If time travel was real and men and women of past history could see the advances that we have made, it would seem magical to them, but I doubt that even humans of recent past would be even remotely proud of what has become of this soft generation, especially men.

We are weaker because of all these comforts, but we got some cool stuff—stuff we never thought possible. Interesting how we think of all these incredible ideas of things to make, and even still, everything your eyes see every day was made out of material that just so happened to be here in the earth—just waiting for man to find it. Higher power? Yeah, He's higher power. He is *God*, the great "I Am."

Our puny minds think that we have an original thought and guess what? Everything that we thought possible was indeed possible because of what some "higher power" placed here for us to find. Or is it all some big wondrous accident? You are smarter than that, this was no accident, we are no accident. Scientists today are smart, and they have had to admit that there is indeed "intelligent design", well thank you detective obvious. "Intelligent design" is still another way of not giving God His credit. The Lord Almighty is His name or you can call Him by one of His other names, He has many. We should also not swear on Him. He is our Father and is due our respect in every way. It's hysterical that today's "smart men" denounce God. Are they not smart enough to have put two and two together yet?

Here's the answer for you: anything and everything man has ever built was built from the materials here in the earth that man is not responsible for. It was and is here. We can think of an amazing thing, like a house to live in with electricity and plumbing and cool air and hot air. How about a horseless carriage? Then we fly. We will call it a plane because it flies over a plane. Microwave ovens. Hey, let's make it so we can share all we want to with an entire world with a little device we can hold in our hand. The gadgets, the cars, the stuff. We keep expanding a mind that we didn't give to ourselves, and whatever cool thing we can think of, well, heck, let's use this material we found in the earth to turn our new ideas into stuff. Indeed, there is a God.

We keep advancing year after year and the materials in the ground keep up the pace with our imagination. What a grand coincidence that it all just happened to be there. It is no coincidence; we need to give *God* his due respect. Let us not be arrogant fools. The Bible is indeed infallible. God made all this.

He also gave us His Word, and He gave part of Himself to us in the Holy Spirit that lives inside of all believers. He gave His son, and we won't even give Him the benefit of doubt about what He says we live in. He wrote of all the wondrous things that He did in the world, and it was verified by us humans and put it to word through incredible men as the Holy Spirit guided their hands. Why God chose that way to do it, I don't know. Using us, corrupt man, to be used as the tools of God Himself to write down His holy words. He is still working that way today, using flawed men to tell other flawed men that there is indeed a Father who loves you, who made you, who gave you an opportunity to experience life. There are lot of dead babies that didn't get that chance. You're here, and you're not dead yet so you have choices to make. You have read this book up to this point. What will you do with your choices?

Yes, we are smart, but mankind are liars. We have made things that we never thought we would see in our lifetime. But we did not go to the moon. "They" will never ever give that one up; it's too big a lie. It ties in with the round earth. They are one and the same. This "level water thing" is a problem. Look the other way masses, so we dutifully look the other way. They tell us to stay inside and wear masks, they shut the economy down, then its ok to not wear the masks and a majority of the population concedes. Humans apparently want to be controlled and in fact are okay with it. Human history proves that the masses are always wrong. God always sides with His people, His children, and that is always not the masses. We need to use that smart brain of ours to realize that God does not make mistakes. He will not lie. Look back at the history of our earth. God promised that He would not flood the earth again and indeed has not. We know that He once did because of all the sea evidence found all over drylands, hundreds and hundreds of miles from any ocean. This, and other recorded events found in God's Word prove that God is real, that God loves us, that He in fact did make everything just the way He said He did. We have eyes but do not see.

We don't need anything else to prove our arrogance, but it will be on full display when this debate reaches a fevered pitch. Once the truth is out and people start to question, it will be an all-out chaotic mess—the likes of which politics has never seen. Ugly won't describe it. Violence will ensue, look at the violence that's going on today over much less important issues. Lord, help us. And you know what? He will. Call upon the name of the Lord and be saved. Remember that parting of the Red Sea? The last part of that story is that the storming Egyptians following the Jews had the intent to kill them all. It looked bad for the Jewish people, but the Egyptians were taken out in that same sea that God used to save His people. Last spoiler alert: we win.

It may be tough for quite some time, and you may wonder if you have done the right thing, made the right choice. It may even feel like an entire army is after you. Hold firm, we will prevail. You bought this book and read it and now know you the truth, and now you are responsible for it.

We in America are basically free to do what we want, but like the song says, "Step out of line the man come get you from behind." What if we don't toe the line? What if we don't buy into what the world is offering? When Jesus rebuked the demons that called themselves Legion after forcing them to leave the man that they possessed, He allowed them to enter into some nearby swine and those pigs charged over a cliff to their death. Are we going to follow blindly over a cliff with the rest of the swine? God has always given us a choice—a choice to believe in Him and a choice to reject Him. We have in front of us a choice to either believe His Holy Word or to not believe in His Holy Word. It's pretty black and white. And it will come with a heavy price if we step out of line, so prepare yourself.

The price of being human is that we will get old and our bodies will die. Today our modern medicine has advanced to levels beyond belief, but then again, has it? We still die relatively young, and one out of every one person ends up dead. Those are some sobering stats. As I am writing this, it has just been confirmed that Kobe Bryant, the Laker great, and his daughter and others including almost an entire family has died in a horrible helicopter crash here in California. While this is so very tragic and hard to make sense of, we must know that no person alive has knowledge of when their last day on earth is. Like the Bible says, we are here for but a moment and our life here is but a vapor. *"You don't know what will happen tomorrow. For what is your life? It is even a vapor that appears for a little while and then vanishes away" (James 4:14).* As an older man now, I can clearly bear witness to that fact. While I feel like I'm am still a young man in my mind, the passage of time and a mirror tell a different story. Our bodies are breaking down day by day, minute by minute. We are all in a constant state of dying. We may get sick and die. We may be involved in a horrible accident and die. Some of us will only get ten years, and some a hundred two years. Some are aborted and never get one day. We may live a long life and die comfortably in our bed with lots of loved ones at our side, but we will die.

Eleanor Roosevelt said, "You need to learn from other people's mistakes because you can't live long enough to make them all yourself." We were meant to live forever, we were not meant to die, and if you are saved by the blood of Christ, then you won't die, you will live forever with your Creator. If you are not saved by the blood, then you are not and will not. Eleanor Roosevelt was a wise woman, and we will do well to take her advice and correct our monstrous mistake of buying into the devils lies about what our world looks like. It was said that Kobe and his daughter went to church the morning of the crash. That wasn't a mistake. I bet you that is a decision that neither of them regrets. All the money in the world, all the fame, all the earthy glory stays here on this earth. We need to lay up our treasures in heaven, and we should start by believing every word in the Bible that God gave us.

How proud the Lord must be for all the advances that we have made. He alone is responsible for our keen intellect. We can study and learn and grow, but we did not make the mind. We have mastered so many things, but it seems that most of life's conveniences have been made possible in only the last one hundred years or so. We don't remember the hardships of days gone by. We don't know what it is like to maybe have one horse per family and not being able to travel more than a hundred miles from our home. Cold milk, hot pizza, hair dryers, toothpaste, and toilet paper, and every other conceivable thing that has not always been here has given even the poorest among us a comfortable life. We are soft and spoiled. We are haughty and proud and in need of nothing like a certain church that was mentioned earlier. We need to humble ourselves, be grateful and thankful for all the wondrous things that God has allowed us to have here to make our lives more comfortable. And we need to humble ourselves to accept that we are wrong and that we have been fooled into believing what Satan wants us to believe concerning our world.

Face it, whether you believe in God or not, He is real, and He is indeed a higher power—if you want to call Him that—who gave us all these wondrous things to find. It was no accident. How could it have been? We are the only lifeforms in our habitation that are made in His image, and He made us this wondrous world to live in and gave us all that we would need to survive and grow and make cool stuff with. He gave us an inquisitive mind and a thirst for knowledge that has driven man to create all kinds of incredible things. He gave us the example of parents. Are we not proud of the things that our own children accomplish? I'm sure He is proud of the way we have used our minds to make all of the amazing things that we have today. But at the same time, He gave us guidelines to follow, and we abuse them daily and this does not make Him proud. Every advance we make or new gadget we come up with immediately becomes tainted by Satan and used for his dark purposes. I'm sure that this breaks God's heart. Billions of things to do and a very small list of guidelines to follow, and of course, we can't follow them. If we did follow them, the issue that this book is about would not had to have been written.

He gave us the example of marriage. We each have different roles. The man wants respect from his wife, and the wife wants love from her husband. God having made both male and female obviously has both these fundamental needs as well. I am aware that God has need of nothing, but He does want our love and our respect. That is why He made us. And we disrespect Him by going along with men concerning a moving earth and a still sun. And we curse at Him and do not love Him the way we should. This "higher power" "intelligence" has many names. Quit referring to Him in general as a "higher intelligence." He has plenty of names. I'm sure that you'll find one that you like in this list.

| | | |
|---|---|---|
| Advocate (1 John 2:1) | Almighty (Revelation 1:8) | Alpha (Revelation 1:8) |
| Amen (Revelation 3:14) | Angel of the Lord (Genesis 16:7) | Anointed One (Psalm 2:2) |
| Apostle (Hebrews 3:1) | Author and Perfecter of our faith (Hebrews 12:2) | Beginning (Revelation 21:6) |
| Bishop of souls (1 Peter 2:25) | Branch (Zechariah 3:8) | Bread of life (John 6:35, 48) |
| Bridegroom (Matthew 9:15) | Carpenter (Mark 6:3) | Chief Shepherd (1 Peter 5:4) |
| The Christ (Matthew 1:16) | Comforter (Jeremiah 8:18) | Consolation of Israel (Luke 2:25) |
| Cornerstone (Ephesians 2:20) | Dayspring (Luke 1:78) | Day Star (2 Peter 1:19) |
| Deliverer (Romans 11:26) | Desire of Nations (Haggai 2:7) | Emmanuel (Matthew 1:23) |
| End (Revelation 21:6) | Everlasting Father (Isaiah 9:6) | Faithful and True Witness (Revelation 3:14) |
| First Fruits (1 Corinthians 15:23) | Foundation (Isaiah 28:16) | Fountain (Zechariah 13:1) |
| Friend of sinners (Matthew 11:19) | Gate for the sheep (John 10:7) | Gift of God (2 Corinthians 9:15) |
| God (John 1:1) | Glory of God (Isaiah 60:1) | Good Shepherd (John 10:11) |
| Governor (Matthew 2:6) | Great Shepherd (Hebrews 13:20) | Guide (Psalm 48:14) |
| Head of the Church (Colossians 1:18) | High Priest (Hebrews 3:1) | Holy one of Israel (Isaiah 41:14) |
| Horn of salvation (Luke 1:69) | I Am (Exodus 3:14) | Jehovah (Psalm 83:18) |
| Jesus (Matthew 1:21) | King of Israel (Matthew 27:42) | King of Kings (1 Timothy 6:15) |

| | | |
|---|---|---|
| Lamb of God (John 1:29) | Last Adam (1 Corinthians 15:45) | Life (John 11:25) |
| Light of the world (John 8:12;John 9:5) | Lion of the tribe of Judah (Revelation 5:5) | Lord of Lords (1 Timothy 6:15) |
| Master (Matthew 23:8) | Mediator (1 Timothy 2:5) | Messiah (John 1:41) |
| Mighty God (Isaiah 9:6) | Morning Star (Revelation 22:16) | Nazarene (Matthew 2:23) |
| Omega (Revelation 1:8) | Passover Lamb (1 Corinthians 5:7) | Physician (Matthew 9:12) |
| Potentate (1 Timothy 6:15) | Priest (Hebrews 4:15) | Prince of Peace (Isaiah 9:6) |
| Prophet (Acts 3:22) | Propitiation (1 John 2:2) | Purifier (Malachi 3:3) |
| Rabbi (John 1:49) | Ransom (1 Timothy 2:26) | Redeemer (Isaiah 41:14) |
| Refiner (Malachi 3:2) | Refuge (Isaiah 25:4) | Resurrection (John 11:25) |
| Righteousness (Jeremiah 23:6) | Rock (Deuteronomy 32:4) | Root of David (Revelation 22:16) |
| Rose of Sharon (Song of Solomon 2:1) | Ruler of God's creation (Revelation 3:14) | Sacrifice (Ephesians 5:2) |
| Savior (2 Samuel 22:47) | Second Adam (1 Corinthians 15:47) | Seed of Abraham (Galatians 3:16) |
| Seed of David (2 Timothy 2:8) | Seed of the woman (Genesis 3:15) | Servant (Isaiah 42:1) |
| Shepherd (1 Peter 2:25) | Shiloh (Genesis 49:10) | Son of David (Matthew 15:22) |
| Son of God (Luke 1:35) | Son of Man (Matthew 18:11) | Son of Mary (Mark 6:3) |
| Son of the Most High (Luke 1:32) | Stone (Isaiah 28:16) | Sun of Righteousness (Malachi 4:2) |
| Teacher (Matthew 26:18) | Way (John 14:6) | Wonderful Counselor (Isaiah 9:6) |
| Word (John 1:1) | Vine (John 15:1) | Truth (John 14:6) |

Truth was intentionally placed last on the list. Jesus said, "*I am the Way, the Truth, and the Life. No one comes to the Father except through Me.*" *(John 14:6)*

God is truth. In Him, there are no lies and no deception. And His last name is not "Dammit."

# CHAPTER 16

# No Turning Back

*And God spoke all these words, saying: "I am the Lord your God, who brought you out of the land of Egypt, out of the house of bondage. You shall have no other gods before Me."*

—*Exodus 20:1–3*

1. Don't have other gods before me.
2. Don't make images to bow down before them.
3. Don't take the Lords name in vain.
4. Keep the Sabbath holy.
5. Honor you father and mother.
6. Don't kill.
7. Don't commit adultery.
8. Don't steal.
9. Don't lie.
10. Don't covet.

Did you know all of these by heart? Don't worry if you didn't, most people can't recite them all. Although, most people know a lot of useless information like words to songs or the name of all the Beatles. It's what's important to us, right? The order is important as well. The first four have to do with God and the last six have to do with us. The perfect 10.

1.  Don't have other gods before me. Notice that "gods" is not capitalized. There are no other gods but that which man makes up in his mind and puts first before the only God. What are we putting first in our thoughts about our world? That it's round and moving, contrary to what the Bible clearly says.

2.  Don't make images to bow down before them. Well, what is a globe? I just visited my former church not too long ago, and as I walked into the office to see one of my old pastors, there it was. A globe sitting out on the only table in the front office displayed in a prominent spot so that everyone who walked in would see it. A globe is a carved image that the world worships and will not let go of at any cost.

3.  Don't take the Lord's name in vain. This commandment does not mean using God's name as a swear word (although I absolutely abhor that). It does mean, that taking away what God said He did and made and changing it to what we want it to say and mean, is lying about God and His miracles. That is taking God's name in vain.

4.  Keep the Sabbath holy. God created in six days and rested on the seventh. He didn't need the rest. This was a model for us to follow—work six days and rest on the seventh. By resting on the seventh day, we show respect for God and the creation that He made. By denying His handiwork and making a moving sun a still sun, we do not show our respect and appreciation for what He actually made for us. Therefore, we do not keep the Sabbath holy because we call God a liar by insisting that the world spins and the sun does not move. We do this every day of the week including the Sabbath.

5.  Honor you father and mother. If your father and mother do not believe in God's Word the way that it has been revealed to you, then your parents cause you to choose God and His

Word over their rule. God wins every time in that scenario. Honor your father and mother, but if they teach against the Word of God, then you must honor God. And God said that the sun moves and the earth is stationary. And He is the ultimate Father.

6. Don't kill. Taking away the fact that we are indeed special and making us just some orbiting "planet" among many other "planets" strikes at the very heart of this commandment. If we are not special, then we are an accident like the world preaches with the Big Bang theory and evolution. We are not held to an accountable God and therefore can "do as thy wilt" including murder and any other sin, which in a world without morality, and God would not be condemned.

7. Don't commit adultery. Cheating on your wife or husband, yes. Cheating on God? We wouldn't dare! Or would we? Cheating and lying are the same thing. If you cheat, you lie. We cheat God out of His glory by denying what He made and how He made it. We also do the same thing with abortion; we take something as incredible as a human life and make it worthless (see number 6). We are not worthless; we are made in His image but unfortunately, we commit adultery on a grand scale daily.

8. Don't steal. While this commandment will keep us out of jail here on earth, are we not stealing from God by claiming that we are a big accident? That He didn't really make us and our unique world? This is stealing His glory and making it our own by insisting that the world is one way when God says it's another way.

9. Don't lie. This one doesn't need defining. The globe model earth and a stationary sun is indeed a direct lie and in total contradiction to the Bible.

10. Don't covet. The world has a moving earth and a stationary sun. We don't want to be singled out as being stupid. We covet the acceptance of the world, so we go along with

what is in total opposition to God's Word. Guilty here as well.

And just as a reminder, these are not guidelines. They are commandments.

What is your God? What will you defend passionately? Remember, the masses are always wrong so choose wisely who you will serve today.

The masses were wrong about God's wrath and the flood that came.

The masses were wrong about God's plan to free them from Egypt.

The masses were wrong about wanting Barabbas over Jesus.

The masses were wrong about slavery.

The German masses were wrong about Hitler.

The masses are wrong about their understanding of the Bible and what will get you to heaven.

The masses are wrong about a stationary sun and a moving earth planet.

> *"Though they join forces, the wicked will not go unpunished" (Proverbs 11:21).*

This higher power, "God," left us an instruction book, the Bible, and told us that no one is too tamper with it, and what happened? Yup, we tampered with it big time. The NIV does not read like the King James or the New King James. God warned us just like He warned Adam and Eve, and we did it anyway, didn't we? We had to mess with His words and change them. The first man sinned by eating the forbidden fruit. Was there really a forbidden fruit? Maybe. I argue that there was nothing magical at all about that fruit. God just showed us one thing we couldn't have, and we couldn't resist the temptation. God caused their eyes to be opened not because they ate the fruit but because they sinned by disobeying Him. He gave us billions of things to do and just one thing not to do and we did it. We needed a lesson from our Father. So unfortunately for all of humanity, we were disciplined, and now we live in a world where Satan can tempt us to believe in something and to go along with it just because everyone else does. Satan has done such a masterful job of it that just asking the question "Does the sun move?" makes you sound stupid.

Like Adam, we were given billions of things to do and a couple of things we are not to do in the ten commandments, and we have not done well. Well, you will definitely have the temptation to agree with the world about a moving and spinning earth. It's common knowledge, and to go against it will cause you trouble that you don't want. Heck, I don't want the trouble, but because of this biblical truth we have just been exposed to, trouble is coming in a way that nobody is ready for. You don't want to be singled out. You don't want to be ostracized by society. You don't want to be called ignorant. You don't want to lose your job or friends and family, and reputation. Too bad! Grow up and prepare yourself like a man. The end times are here, and you will have to make a decision.

*What does it profit a man if he gains the whole world but loses his soul? (Matthew 16:26)*

We have comforts, we have money, we have food and vacations—we really have need of nothing if we think about it. If we are willing to work hard to obtain these things, they are attainable. But we feel empty when we get these things. They did not bring us the lasting happiness that we seek. The shiny toys fade and the new car smell goes away and gets a dent in the door and we long for another vacation. We look up to famous singers and actors and sports heroes and want what they have, but how many times do we see them fall? They seem to have everything, but what do they really have? If we have God, then we have all that we need.

This is a very short life. Do not spend it trying to attain things that don't matter. Find a way to make money and support your family. This is biblical, for a man who does not work should not eat. But also live daily on the Word of God. It does not fade. The new smell does not go away, and there are no dents and no mistakes. His Word is true now and forever. Because He said that the sun moves, then trust that it does move. You and I are not God. We are not smarter than the Creator of all. Over the course of time, the fact that the sun moves and the earth does not will become common knowledge, and we will feel silly for ever believing different. Mankind will slowly wake up and realize that we have all been sold a bill of goods from the devil himself. It already has been proven by the Word of God, we are just too arrogant and prideful to admit it. The earth has always stood still, and the sun has always moved whether or not we humans accept it.

There are over three hundred thousand churches in America. Over the course of two hundred and forty-four years of Americas existence, these churches must have had at least five pastors each (a very low guess). Regardless, even at that rate, we have had at least 1.5 million pastors and most likely a lot more that have come and gone through the pulpits of these American churches.

It is the job and life calling of these men to lead the church of Christ. I believe that most of these men are sincere in their love of the Lord God. They study and they prepare their messages for each Sunday, they visit the sick and dying, they do God's work—of that I am sure. Sharing God's Word and leading lost sinners to salvation through Christ is a privilege and a joy. Being a pastor and leading God's people must be an extraordinarily tough but rewarding job—and one that I cannot relate to. Having said that, no one can tell me with a straight face that these millions of pastors, deacons, elders, members, and others have missed this crucial information about the movement of the sun that is found throughout almost every book in the Bible. This is highly doubtful, which means one of two things. They are ignorant at best, or at worst, they are intentionally misleading the flock of Christ! Well, now what do they say? Will sermons now be preached about the lies of the world? Will minds be challenged? What will be the world's reaction? We've already spelled that out.

*"'The light is near,' they say, 'in the face of darkness.' The innocent stirs himself up against the hypocrite. And he who has clean hands will be stronger and stronger. My spirit however is broken, my days almost gone."* This is taken from *Job 17*. I am indeed not a pastor nor an elder or a deacon. I have no authority or standing in this world or in the church to help my cause, but I do have the wisdom and peace given to me by God. I have a loving wife and family, and most importantly, I have the Word of God and that is all the authority anyone needs. Most importantly the Word tells us that Jesus our Savior is coming back and we will want to be found as having fought the good fight.

My wife and I have been married for over thirty years. We raised three beautiful humans who have since all been married and multiplied. We still all go to church together every Sunday for some thirty years in a row. We love our church family but what kind of day do we live in that we cannot speak against the accepted normal or ask an obvious question? Or challenge our leaders? Every word you've have read in this book has made perfect sense (because the words are from the Bible. They are God's words).

God's Word and God's natural laws have been proven, yet here we are. We doubt, and even people who think that they are open-minded and consider themselves as to having the keys to heaven because of their personal relationship with Jesus the Christ will still not be able to consider the fact that they, along with "the masses" are wrong, God's Word is right 100 percent—no exceptions. He gave His Word to us, and He gave His Word for us.

I am not naïve, you don't get to call out the devil himself and try to break the spell that he has over the church today without consequences. And who dares to call out men of God? I am intentionally stepping on the toes of those at the top because it has not been done and needs to be. But who the flip am I to think that something this huge was given to me by reading the Bible? *Gospel Earth* can call out Satan because *"greater is He who is in me than he who is in the world" (1 John 4:4)*. This gives me and you all the authority we would need. As born-again Christians we have the actual Spirit of

God inside us. So, *"we can do all things through Christ who gives us strength" (Philippians 4:13).*

I'm a nobody in the high arch of biblical knowledge. I'm no Billy Graham. I am a simple man who read the Word of God just like you, I am not special except that I am a child of the Most High. I seek no glory and to be quite honest I would be shaking in my boots over this except for the fact that God has assured me that I should have no fear of anyone who can kill the body but not the soul. That is His job.

Finally, my brothers and sisters in Christ, be watchful. The signs of the times are upon us and they are real and this will be the issue that will bring the end of days. Think about it. If you truly believe what the Bible says about everything in every story, in every word, then you have to see that the Bible is correct in stating unequivocally that the sun moves and that the earth does not, and that changes everything. The worlds precious "gravity" theory falls apart immediately with a moving sun. After that, everything else breaks down. No "gravity"—no gravitational pull, no spinning planets, no spinning at all. You see, if the sun moves (and it does) and the earth does not (and it doesn't), then the earth is not a globe. If it were, then half of that globe would always be in complete darkness.

Zero argument.

Satan has pulled off whoppers of lies throughout history. He is the cause of all this. He takes God's awesome display of power and wonder and turns it into the opposite of what God intended. It has been said that *"an honest man who is shown to be wrong must either admit his error or cease to be honest."* Defend the Word of God and fight the just war against Satan and his minions and be free. Come, Lord Jesus.

In a nutshell, asking a Christian to deny what God's Word clearly says is like asking us to deny Jesus the Christ, the maker of all we see, touch, feel, smell, love, and enjoy. He has given us our very breath, He has hung upon a cross and died a vicious death for us, and we have the gall to believe something other than what His Word says. Lovers of God's Word who have embraced the truths laid out here in the preceding pages can never be brought back into the lie. This is scary to the world, and they will not accept it. All the truth, all the facts, all the science, all the verses in the Bible will be tossed aside to save, "the religion of a round spinning planet", and only he or she who has ears can hear.

There is an old song that we sang back in the 1970s. We used it as an altar call most of the time. Here are the words. They are simple but convicting. Sing along as you remember the tune.

> *I have decided to follow Jesus. I have decided to follow Jesus. I have decided to follow Jesus, no turning back, no turning back.*
>
> *Though none go with me, I still will follow. Though none go with me, I still will follow. Though none go with me, I still will follow, no turning back, no turning back.*
>
> *The cross before me, the world behind me. The cross before me, the world behind me. The cross before me, the world behind me, no turning back, no turning back.*
>
> *What have you decided?*

# FINAL THOUGHTS

M y intent is not to attack our ministers, deacons, elders, or members. I sincerely believe that the hearts of our pastors and leaders are in the right place, along with the right motives. However, after reading many commentaries regarding the passage in *Joshua 10:13*; it is evident that rather than acknowledging another miracle of God, many pastors found it easier to go along with the world and hypothesize away the fact that the sun moves. Unfortunately if this is your belief as well then you too have denied one of God's miracles. Please be reminded, Joshua spoke to the Lord and said, "*Sun stand still*"…"*So the sun stood still*", as a matter of fact, that Bible passage repeats itself in the same verse "*So the sun stood still in the midst of heaven, and did not hasten to go down for about a whole day. And there has been no day like that, before it or after it, that the Lord heeded the voice of man*". When the Bible repeats itself you can trust that there is no mistake. Furthermore, this is not an isolated verse about the movement of the sun, *Gospel Earth* has listed many verses from our Christian Bible supporting God's amazing creation and how He made it work. I spoke with pastors and leaders throughout our country, either in person or over the phone, and a common theme when asked about the moving sun was this: "I never really thought about it." This concerns me greatly. Obviously, with this book, I have thought a lot about it. I wanted answers, instead what I got was highly respected men of God side stepping obvious biblical truths. Why is the miracle about a moving sun dismissed as a non-miracle and all the other miracles are accepted at face value? Maybe the water was always wine. Maybe no one walked on water, maybe there was a sand bar or some conveniently placed stones just below the water level so it appeared as if Jesus and Peter defied physics. Did Lots wife actually turn to a pillar of salt or was that just poetic imagery? Was Moses seeing things when he saw a burning bush that was not consumed? A virgin birth? Did Jesus really die for us? Maybe He just healed up on His own in the tomb and wasn't really dead! We know that the answer to the question is this: by acknowledging that the sun was stopped, reason dictates that one must also acknowledge the movement of the sun, and that can't be allowed, as it blows up the "almighty gravity" which in turn cascades into exposing every other lie, it all falls apart. We can deny the just read miracles, and with this kind of reasoning easily dismiss everyone of God's miracles with conjecture and speculation and thereby undermine the Bible and our Christian faith. Or, we can believe what God has plainly spelled out in scripture. He does not lie, He is never wrong, His miracles are true and verified. The sun moves. It's in the Bible, your senses are correct, and true science proves it all. Amen.

*"And it shall come to pass in that day," says the Lord God,*
*"That I will make the sun go down at noon, and I will*
*darken the earth in broad daylight." (Amos 8:9)*

# ABOUT THE AUTHOR

S teven Patrick is a husband to his wife of thirty-three years, a father of two daughters, a son, and Papa to seven grandchildren. Having raised his family at a young age, he was able to semi-retire and venture into new projects. As a business owner, musician, and now author, Steven seeks to be the very best he can be in every area of his life. Of all his titles, being a born-again Christian is the most important role in his life. Being driven by the Holy Spirit to write on a topic that few others would dare, he felt a strong calling to begin writing about the Word of God. With a love for the lost, Steven prays that they would find faith and that the faithful would have their eyes opened up to the deceptions that have been accepted as truths in our world today. Steven Patrick is a man of God and a forever student of the Lord's infallible word. *"Only fools hate knowledge"* (*Proverbs 1:22*).